DANGEROUS PLAYGROUND

Books by Drew Kizer

Christian Hope

Christian Faith

The Cast of the Cross

From Conquerors to Kings

From Captives to Christ

Wisdom's Call

Make Your Stand

DANGEROUS PLAYGROUND

The Christian and Social Media

by Drew Kizer

DANGEROUS PLAYGROUND
The Christian and Social Media

Published by Riddle Creek Publishing
320 Spring Cove Rd.
Florence, AL 35634
www.riddlecreekpublishing.com

ISBN: 978-0-9835009-0-2

TABLE OF CONTENTS

PREFACE

Music used to cost money. Kids went to these places called record stores to purchase little black discs called records, seven inches, ten inches, or twelve inches in diameter. When they got home, they placed the discs on a machine called a record player, or turntable. The machine turned the records under a needle, producing vibrations carried by the system into external speakers that played music for the listeners. You can still find these strange black discs in the closets of eccentric music lovers who can't let go of the past (I have a large collection at home).

After records came cassette tapes (I'm sparing you an excursus on the eight-track). Magnetic tape turned on two spools that fed electromagnets, or heads, that rendered the magnetic field produced by the tape into sound. With the advent of the cassette, music became portable. People no longer had to wait on disc jockeys at radio stations to play their favorite songs. They could push a cassette into the stereo in their dashboard and listen to anything from their personal collection. Another innovation of the cassette tape was the ability to record music onto a blank tape from another source, such as a record, or the radio, or another tape. People started sharing mixtapes with one another. Music has always had a way of bringing people together. Mixtapes added yet another layer of socialization.

CDs (compact discs) are still lurking in the back corners of the electronic departments of retail stores. Lighter than their vinyl cousins, they hold more music – up to about 80 minutes. CD players decode the music stored digitally on CDs by tracing a laser across the surface of the disc. Like tapes, CDs are portable, so you can listen to your favorite bands in your car, assuming you bought their latest album, or at least ripped it off of your friend and burned a copy using your computer.

By the 1990s, personal computers were quickly becoming a fixture in every home. As with cassette tapes, kids were now sharing music on CDs, but music sharing required a lot of effort: You would have to buy the CD, download it to your computer, organize the music files using computer software, and burn the music to a blank CD purchased from the store. Once you made it through this process, the results were a vast improvement over music copied to cassette tapes, but the whole routine was a chore. Some people just listened to the music on their computers. Also, MP3 players (replaced by iPods and then smartphones) found their way into the market. Music fans uploaded files to these small devices they carried in their pockets and listened through their headphones. People began to bypass all forms of physical media – records, cassette tapes, and CDs. Now that they were listening to music straight from their computers, they began to wonder, "What if I could share my favorite songs through the internet?"

An answer to this question surfaced on June 1, 1999, in the form of a revolutionary online platform called Napster developed by two young programmers, Shawn Fanning and Sean Parker.[1] Napster enabled users to share their music online using a new technology called "peer to peer file sharing" (P2P), which made downloading files more efficient. Not only that, because users were sharing files from their personal libraries, the music was free. Also, the files were coming from the eclectic collections of young music fans, making almost any recording available, even rare bootlegs. Music fans were no longer limited to whatever was in stock at their local music store. They could listen to anything that they wanted without having to pay a dime for it.

Napster had other features in addition to filesharing. Users could download the software and open an account for free. It also combined an audio library with a music player, something we take for granted now through iTunes and Spotify.[2] The transfer window displayed the progress of uploads and downloads, which heightened anticipation of the file sharers. While internet relay chat and AOL Instant Messenger had been around for years, Napster was unique in that it incorporated chat into the sharing of *music*, a form of information. Extremely popular, Napster amassed 80 million accounts in less than two years.[3]

Social media has always been about two things: socializing and information gathering.[4] According to these criteria, Napster was an early precursor to the social media platforms we now know and love. MySpace would not come along for another four years. Facebook launched in 2004, and YouTube went public in 2005. Twitter, Snapchat, and Instagram would not see the light of day for several more years.

There was one problem. Napster did not have the legal right to aid in the distribution of copyrighted material. Its famous icon, a devil wearing headphones, did not help matters. Artists began to sue. The courts got involved, and the service was officially shut down in 2001. Napster still exists in some form, but the original version that allowed users to download music for free no longer exists. That does not mean it did not leave its mark. There is the time before Napster and the time after. People still pay for music, but not like they used to. Artists complain that they no longer make much money from recording (Taylor Swift earned around $300,000 for her song "Shake It Off" in 46.3 million streams, according to one report[5]). If you want to make a living in the music industry today, you have to go on tour. How do recording artists attract fans to their concerts? By music streamed online through platforms like iTunes, Google Play, and Spotify, programs that took their cue from Napster.

Did MySpace and Facebook get the idea for social networking from Napster? Not likely. Earlier examples of social networking like SixDegrees and Friendster predate Napster, but they were not very popular.[6] The pioneer of free music was the first online service of its kind to attract 80 million users. And no wonder. Music has a way of bringing people together. At the very least, we can say that in its brief existence, perched at the turn of the century, Napster was on the cusp of a social media revolution.

Generation Z

Now we take social media for granted. Enough time has passed for a generation to emerge that cannot remember a time before there was social media. Born between 1995 and 2012, members of this demographic are called Generation Z. Jean Twenge, a psychologist at San Diego State University who has done extensive research into this generation, calls it "iGen." The oldest members of this generation were young adolescents when the iPhone was introduced and high school students when the iPad hit the shelves. It is a rather large group, making up 24 percent of the U.S. population.

The research on Gen Z reveals that it is very different from previous generations:[7]

- Members of Gen Z are "smartphone natives," meaning they grew up with smartphones and do not remember a time before the internet.
- Three out of four own an iPhone. Some studies estimate this number as high as 80 percent.
- On average, they spend nine hours a day online, including streaming music and video. Two of those nine hours are consumed on social media.
- The average age a Gen Z'er gets his first smartphone in the U.S. is ten.
- Gen Z shows a disturbing trend of secularization. About one in four do not attend religious services or practice any form of spirituality.
- They also perceive one another through fractured bits. They have gotten good at taking fragments from social media, like images, texts, and tweets, and putting them together like a puzzle to figure out the whole person.

- On a more positive note, they are more socially active than previous generations. Using their social media tools, they organize marches, speak up for the less fortunate, and fight for a better world. However, Gen Z's armchair activism is a departure from the protests of the 1960s when you could get arrested for sitting at the front of a bus or refusing to leave your seat at a lunch counter. Today's social justice warriors fight their battles in the comfort and safety of their bedrooms.

While many benefits have emerged through the rise of social media, many disturbing trends have also reared their ugly heads. Social media can be a lot of fun, but it is a dangerous playground, and we are fools if we do not proceed carefully.

Much has changed. That is why I am writing this book. Christians need to be aware of the new environment social media has created. You may not personally use social media much; you may not even have an account. It doesn't matter. Social networking has changed the world, and we must prepare ourselves to live righteously in our strange new surroundings.

PART ONE

SOCIAL
STUDIES

CHAPTER ONE

THE SOCIETAL IMPACT OF SOCIAL MEDIA

The summer after my senior year in college was the last time I found myself untethered from all obligations. I had finished school and would not start my new job for another month. Four of my friends were in the same position, and we had the idea of packing a tent, borrowing my dad's minivan and camper, and heading out west for two weeks to see new territory. I was amazed that my parents gave me permission to go. This was before cell phones and GPS. We were planning to drive thousands of miles into unknown territory equipped with only a Rand McNally map and a lust for adventure. The only contact we would have with family would be through payphones. I will never forget that trip. My friends and I experienced the feeling of leaving our ordinary lives behind, even if it was just for two weeks, and finding ourselves in the beauty of God's creation.

I am glad that I had the opportunity to go on that trip when I did because such excursions are impossible today. I do not mean it is impossible to drive out west in your dad's beat up minivan. If anything, it is easier to journey to new and unknown places, but the navigational tools and connectivity available on our smartphones make trips easier and, shall I say, less adventurous. Trips are supposed to involve a little mystery and risk. It's as Bilbo told Frodo in J.R.R. Tolkien's *The Lord of the Rings*: "It's a dangerous business, Frodo, going out of your door.... You step into the Road, and if you don't keep your feet, there is no knowing where you might be swept off to."[8] Not knowing what you are about to experience is part of the adventure of travel, or it used to be.

It is impossible to get lost today. It would be crazy for me to complain about technology's advances, as if they were not helpful. I love not having to get directions. It's nice to be able to drive to a new city armed with nothing but my smartphone. But adventures into the great unknown are important. We have become a people without quests, and our lost adventures have threatened something precious to our ability to discover ourselves and learn more about our place in this world.

The world has changed. What has changed it? Has the introduction of social media transformed us? It's not that simple. Social media has been the way people have shared information for most of human history. In the Roman Empire, senators passed along news and gossip on papyri. Early Christians during that time copied and distributed Paul's epistles from church to church. During the Reformation, the printing press helped Martin Luther and his supporters tackle corruptions in the Roman Catholic Church through a grassroots movement. And in seventeenth century Europe, scientists, artists, and philosophers gathered in coffee houses to learn the latest developments. It was not until the mid-nineteenth century, with the advent of the steam powered printing press, followed by radio and television in the twentieth century, that ideas and information began to spread by means of "mass media," information distributed by a few centralized sources, like governments, broadcast companies, and newspapers.[9]

With the advent of new technologies, the world is returning to a system of social networking in which information is chain-copied and passed on by the people, to the people. One benefit of this system is that corrupt institutions cannot control the information as easily as they could in the last century. On the other hand, nowadays everything gets out. Information is free and plentiful, but it is not vetted by any universally accepted source. That means we have to be more discerning than ever before.

Social media is not new. The *technology* is new. Now that we have returned to a system in which the people, not institutions, control the flow of information, we are copying and sharing knowledge at rates that were unthinkable fifty years ago. The speed and access have freed us from the restraints of the physical media of the past, enabling us to spread earth-shattering news, or trivial information about everyday life, in a matter of seconds.

The benefits of modern technology are obvious: more information at our fingertips, connectivity, social networking, creativity tools, universal navigation, and endless entertainment. But while we have enjoyed the seemingly limitless possibilities afforded by new technology, have we stopped to ask how it is changing our world?

Stunted Growth

Young people are growing up more slowly these days. People used to be on their own by the age of 18, but adulthood comes much later these days. One indication of this cultural shift is the change in healthcare laws in 2010 allowing young adults to stay on their parents' health insurance until the age of 26. The late blooming is spreading to other areas, as well. Teenagers are getting their driver's licenses later, working less to earn money, moving out later, and getting married and having families at an older age. They are going out less and interacting with society less because their social lives are lived on their phones. In the words of Jean Twenge, "18-year-olds now act more like 15-year-olds used to, and 15-year-olds more like 13-year-olds. Childhood now stretches well into high school."[10] Social media plays a big role in this protraction of childhood. It is taking away our innocence at a younger age without giving young people the tools they need to grow up.[11]

11

Information

Since social media is driven by networking, it has become a source of information for many people. We can learn about anything, from a good lasagna recipe to the number for a reliable plumber. Reports show that 62 percent of Americans get their news from social media.[12] We network to learn about politics, local news, recreational events, hobbies, commercial interests, and religious and philosophical views.

Because of its potential for sharing information, social media has become very important in political campaigns. Just as television influenced the outcome of the presidential campaign in 1960, apps like Facebook and Twitter have a tremendous impact on U.S. elections today. For example, during the 2016 presidential election, President Trump's campaign hired a political data firm named Cambridge Analytica to harvest the private information of more than 50 million Facebook users. The firm provided Trump's campaign with tools to identify the personalities of voters and influence their behavior.[13] Facebook has since changed their policies to prevent this kind of data mining in the future for political purposes, but what new strategies will politicians find to use social media to influence our minds?

Corrupt people are always looking for ways to exploit these powerful tools. Presidential campaigns were not the only organizations interested in influencing the U.S. elections in 2016. We now know that Russians used social media to spread false information, propaganda, and viral pages. It has been estimated that 126 million Facebook users saw Russian posts containing disinformation intended to influence the election.[14] Fake news is real. You cannot trust the internet.

Social media bills itself as a free market for information sharing, but in some ways it is making us dumber.[15] Facebook, for example, analyzes the people and stories you pay attention to and adjusts your newsfeed so that you hear more and more often from the same small set of sources. If you know how this works, you can fight this narrowing of your exposure with self-awareness, purposely going outside your usual sources for information to broaden your horizons.[16] Most of us do not have the energy to develop strategies to outsmart Facebook's algorithms. We log on to click away in numbness, not knowing how the information we are reading pushed its way in front of equally relevant news we might never see.

You cannot even know for sure whether you are interacting with real people. Trend setters on social media invent users out of whole cloth, aggravating the public's desire for truth. Jaron Lanier describes these false personas as "bots, AIs, agents, fake reviewers, fake friends, fake followers, fake posters, automated catfishers: a menagerie of wraiths."[17] Dr. Frankenstein could only make one monster in his castle. He would have a field day online, with infinite potential to make his creatures live. For example, on Twitter Russian hackers used bots (software programs imitating human behavior on the internet) in over 400,000 accounts used for political discourse during the 2016 presidential debates.[18] That was enough to alter the online discourse and influence reporters to write inaccurate reports, which in turn undermined the credibility of the news while simultaneously spreading false information to the public.[19]

Some corrupt organizations abuse social media by distributing information. Others, like totalitarian governments, *restrict* information. Social media gives a voice to oppressed populations who would not otherwise be able to speak out. Corrupt governments that want to keep a stranglehold on their populations see that as a threat. China and North Korea, for example, are always at the top of the lists of countries who ban social networking sites such as Facebook and Twitter.[20]

One of the biggest societal changes social media has brought about is an influx of information without any way to vet it. People have to decide for themselves if they are reading fact or fiction. On the one hand, important news that might have been suppressed in the past can get out in the open. But on the other, we do not always know if the news we are reading is reliable.

Faith

Andrew Conrad reports:[21]

- More than 70 percent of nonprofit communicators consider social media one of their most important communication channels.
- Almost 85 percent of churches use Facebook.
- 54 percent of Christian millennials watch online videos about faith or spirituality.
- 62 percent of churches use social networking to connect with individuals outside of their congregation. While an even larger number—73 percent according to LifeWay Research—use social media to interact with their congregation, the majority of churches with an online presence are already using social media as a growth tool.
- 65 percent of Americans prefer an in-person preacher to a video sermon. About one third (35 percent) have no preference between live or video sermons, but less than 1 percent prefer a video sermon over a live sermon.

Many pastimes, obligations, and activities we used to experience only in the real world have been uploaded to the virtual world (e.g., shopping, correspondence, learning, etc.), but worship can never have a virtual substitute. Tony Reinke writes,

We must withdraw from our online worlds to gather as a body in our local churches. We gather to be seen, to feel awkward, and perhaps to feel a little unheard and underappreciated, all on purpose. In obedience to the biblical command not to forsake meeting together, we each come as one small piece, one individual member, one body part, in order to find purpose, life, and value in union with the rest of the living body of Christ.[22]

Paul wrote the broken Corinthian church about how they should "come together" (1 Corinthians 11:17-34). Jesus stressed reconciliation in worship, making it a priority to agree with your brothers and sisters (Matthew 5:23-24). We assemble to encourage (Hebrews 11:25) and to live in peace (2 Corinthians 13:11). It's impossible to do all this social heavy-lifting online.

Privacy

Another development brought about by the technological revolution is the disturbing compulsion online users have to share everything about their personal lives. There is a lot of confusion about the difference between what is okay for the public arena and what should be kept private. To be clear, every social media platform sits squarely in the public world, even Snapchat, which promises users that their posts will disappear in seconds. In truth, nothing really disappears. All one has to do is take a screenshot of your snap, and it is archived forever.

Social media users should remember that some secrets can be good. Most of your "friends" on Facebook are complete strangers and have not earned the right to know everything about you. Your dignity is tied to the secrets you keep. Solomon writes, "Whoever guards his mouth preserves his life; he who opens wide his lips comes to ruin" (Proverbs 13:3).

Relationships

Think about how social media has changed the way we look at relationships. We can now "friend" people we have never met. We can "unfriend" someone without suffering any consequences. We can stay connected to others all over the world at all times of the day. It is possible in this new reality to have thousands of followers and yet feel devastatingly alone. Sherry Turkle has coined a phrase that captures this phenomenon: "alone together."[23]

We seem to prefer the company of our smartphones to the people around us. Families sit around tables at restaurants, not talking to each other but glued to their individual electronic devices instead. Devices come before people. If you don't believe me, watch your friend the next time you are together and he gets a phone call or a text message. More than likely, he will interrupt your personal interaction to engage with the virtual world.

The meaning of true relationships is slowly slipping through our hands as we try to replace them online. That is why we increasingly feel alone. The Bible defines friendship as "one who is as your own soul" (Deuteronomy 13:6; 1 Samuel 18:1). Online communication is helpful, but it is fractured. Online, you do not get to know the whole person the way you can in face-to-face interaction.

Empathy

The "selfie" is a perfect symbol for one of the profound ways social media is changing us. We are looking away from the other person and staring at ourselves in the mirror of our phones. The result of this self-obsession is a lack of empathy for others.

On top of the narcissism, the medium of a screen makes it easy for us to forget that a real human being is on the other side, listening to our comments and having an emotional response to them.

Because we are losing empathy, cyberbullying, trolling, vitriol, and callousness are on full display online. This is a serious problem. Rates of teen depression and suicide have skyrocketed since 2011. Generation Z is on the brink of the worst mental health crisis in decades.[24] If we are going to continue to use technology to interact with one another, we have to find a way to sense what others are feeling through our smartphones and computer screens.

A Social Issue

We face an intimidating new world. Technology is not the problem. The problem is how we use the technology to relate to one another. We call it "social media" because the real engine running this information system is relationships—people bumping into each other online like guests at a crowded party, loving and hating, hurting and helping, including and shunning. We face a *social* problem. The technology is just the delivery system.

Sure, things have changed. Change is not always bad. For everything technology has made impossible, there are ten things it has made possible. From distance learning to ordering groceries from an easy chair to networking public transportation, the world offers more opportunities than ever before. We live in an exciting time.

Since this is a social issue, this book is not a manual on how to handle software, smartphones, and networks. Instead, it looks to the Bible for timeless guidance from heaven on how Christians should face this new challenge. God's Word provides the light needed to navigate any territory, even social media (Proverbs 6:20-23). This book asks, "How can a Christian safely stay connected without losing the most important connection – our connection to God?"

DISCUSSION

1. Is social media new? How is information sharing different from the past?

2. Why are teenagers maturing more slowly these days? Is this a problem?

3. Should you be careful about what you read online? How is social media being exploited to influence our minds? What can you do to make sure you are getting the truth?

4. What challenges have new technologies presented the church? Do we relate to one another differently? Can technology replace the assembly?

5. Why should we keep some secrets? How has social media confused the difference between our public and private lives?

6. Explain the meaning of the phrase "alone together."

7. Has the definition of "friend" changed? In what way?

8. What is "empathy"? Why is it important?

9. Is technology a problem in and of itself? What is at the heart of the challenge of social media?

10. How will a Christian stay connected without losing his or her connection to God?

PART TWO

OUR INFINITE APPETITE FOR DISTRACTIONS

CHAPTER TWO

FOCUS

Aldous Huxley noted "man's almost infinite appetite for distractions" in his essay, "Brave New World Revisited."[25] At one time, this insatiable appetite was kept in check by limited technology, but now distractions have been given free reign through continuous online access and its partner, the smartphone. We check our smartphones once every 4.3 minutes of our waking lives.[26] The struggle for attention is a greater challenge than it ever has been before. Sociologist Sherry Turkle says we are in a state of "continual partial attention."[27] Go to any restaurant and you will see families eating around the table, looking down at their individual devices instead of each other. At the coffee shop, one man speaks to a friend who never makes eye contact because he prefers to read a message from another friend who is not there. At the playground, kids cry out to their parents, "Mom, watch this!" while mom scrolls through Facebook. On the bus, nobody talks to one another; they couldn't hear each other if they tried because their ears are stopped up with earbuds that are pumping personalized music from their phones into their heads.

Our ability to concentrate on one thing at a time is extremely important. Focus might be our greatest challenge. We are so distracted! Distracted from prayer, Bible study, helping others, thanking God, counting our blessings, meeting our obligations, attending church services, and many other things. Distractions are even costing lives. In 2016, 3,450 people were killed because they could not keep their eyes on the road.[28] How many other ways does this attention deficit epidemic affect us? In the moment, we do not realize what distraction is doing to us, how it is dividing up the most important moments of our lives and fracturing our dearest relationships. But when we get to the end of our lives, we may look back regretting that we did not have more focus. William James said, "When we reach the end of our days, our life experience will equal what we have paid attention to, whether by choice or default."[29]

Jesus gave us an example of clear-minded focus. That does not mean He never took breaks or that He did not enjoy pastimes. He was human, like us, and knew how to relax. But His overall purpose never left His mind. As He drew closer to the time for which He came into the world, you can see Him getting serious about staying on task. Luke tells us, "When the days drew near for him to be taken up, he set his face to go to Jerusalem" (Luke 9:51). The time for Him to die for the sins of the world was getting closer. Jesus refused to allow anything to distract Him and set His face resolutely towards the city where He would meet His greatest trials. The week of His death, His heavy heart threatened to throw Him off track, but He said, "Now is my soul troubled. And what shall I say? 'Father, save me from this hour'? But for this purpose I have come to this hour" (John 12:27). If Jesus had not kept His focus, the entire human race would be lost!

What kinds of distractions threaten to sidetrack us? How does the Bible describe them?

Dangerous Distractions

Fear of Solitude

We are never alone. Technology has made it possible to stay connected to others continuously. Not only do we want to stay in the loop, we feel a *responsibility* to stay connected, and when we miss a call or fail to respond to a message, we feel badly about it. Increasingly, we feel as though we must have a reason for taking time to be alone and not being available.[30] You don't have to make up an excuse for turning off your phone just to be alone.

It's not wrong. In fact, the Bible teaches that solitude is a very important Christian discipline.

Jesus enjoyed solitude. On numerous occasions, we see Him retreating to the wilderness to get away from the distractions of life to pray. Once, He even ordered His disciples to get into a boat and go to the other side of the Sea of Galilee and "dismissed" the crowds (Matthew 14:22-23; Luke 6:12).

David also was aware of the need for time alone. As a shepherd, he had plenty of time to ponder life and commune quietly with God. Read the following lines from one of his psalms and ask yourself if he would have been able to write them with an iPhone plugged into his ears as he browsed the internet on his laptop:

> When I look at your heavens, the work of your fingers, the moon and the stars, which you have set in place, what is man that you are mindful of him, and the son of man that you care for him? Yet you have made him a little lower than the heavenly beings and crowned him with glory and honor. (Psalm 8:3-5)

Theodore Roosevelt was the embodiment of unyielding optimism and unstoppable energy. Many people would be surprised to learn that Roosevelt dealt with depression his whole life. At the age of 26, after having been married only four years, Roosevelt lost his beloved wife, Alice, who suffered complications in giving birth to their only daughter. In his diary, Roosevelt drew a large X and wrote, "The light has gone out of my life." In his biography on Roosevelt, Edmund Morris wrote that Roosevelt embarked on a trip west to heal. He hungered for solitude. Roosevelt wrote,

> Nowhere, not even at sea, does a man feel more lonely than when riding over the far-reaching, seemingly never

ending plains....Their vastness and loneliness and their melancholy monotony have a strong fascination for him.... Nowhere else does one feel so far off from all mankind....[31]

Roosevelt recognized something that many of us have never learned – that not all aloneness is bad.

Why are we so easily drawn away from solitude by our devices? Maybe we don't understand what solitude is.

Solitude is not loneliness.
Solitude is a state of being geographically alone. Loneliness is a state of being spiritually alone. Philosopher Paul Tillich distinguished the two ideas, pointing out that loneliness expresses "the pain of being alone" and solitude expresses "the glory of being alone."[32] Solitude is not only beneficial; it is essential to a healthy spiritual life. But loneliness is harmful. Jesus enjoyed solitude, but He did not like loneliness (cf. Mark 3:14).

Solitude is not a rejection of the world. A Christian searching for a quiet place to commune with God is not the same thing as a grumpy old hermit looking for a cave to hide in because he hates being around other people.

Solitude is not hiding from your responsibilities. Solitude is periodic, not permanent. If anything, a few quiet moments in solitude increases productivity.

Solitude is not a problem that needs to be solved. We have come to think that unoccupied time is a problem, and our smartphones are the solution. What do you do when you are stopped at a red light? What about when you are in the checkout line at the grocery store? Or waiting for your floor on the elevator? You check your phone. Those few minutes alone in the car are uncomfortable for most of us. But being alone is not the problem. It is a necessary discipline we must develop so that we may grow closer to God.

Solitude is the time and space most conducive to dwelling upon God and what He has done for us.

Perhaps the psalmist said it best when he wrote, "Be still, and know that I am God" (Psalm 46:10). Robert Alter's translation reads, "Let go, and know that I am God." The verb means to relax one's grip on something.[33] In solitude, we release our grip on every distraction that keeps us from giving God our undivided attention. We let go of our anxieties and fears. We release the responsibilities of the day. We give ourselves permission to lose ourselves, if only for a few moments, in prayer and meditation.

The soul needs time and space to breathe. You must retreat from the world to gain perspective and find yourself in relation to God. This is too important to allow something as trivial as a gadget to get in the way.

A Divided Heart

The heart is the control center of every person (Proverbs 4:23). Biblically, the heart is more than the organ that pumps your blood. It is your innermost being, that part of you that does your thinking, feeling and choosing. Therefore, if your heart is distracted, your whole life will be aimless and ineffective. A splintered heart produces a splintered life.

We often praise the art of multitasking, but most of the time, what we call "multitasking" is just a divided heart that cannot focus on what's important in the moment. You cannot study, converse, or pray very well while also texting a friend or checking to see who has just liked your latest post. Smartphone notifications may be the worst enemy of focused concentration today. Just as your mind begins to concentrate on something important, your phone bleeps at you with a personalized signal.

It could be something important, you think. The temptation is too great; you cannot ignore it. You finally give in, pick up your phone again (you just looked at it four minutes ago), and see what is happening on social media. The frequency of these types of distractions are chipping away at our ability to do anything well. Some studies have shown that when you abandon a mental task because of an interruption, recovering focus can take ten to twenty times the length of the interruption.[34] We will never lead productive lives in the digital age unless we learn to control the digital noise competing for our attention. Christians wonder how they will ever find time to study God's Word. We have time; we just don't have the will to focus.

A key phrase defining Caleb's life was that "he wholly followed the Lord." Caleb, along with Joshua, withstood the ten pessimistic spies who said Israel was too weak to inherit the land God had given them. After he and Joshua stood alone against the others, the Lord gave this estimation of him: "... my servant Caleb, because he has a different spirit and has followed me fully, I will bring into the land into which he went, and his descendants shall possess it" (Numbers 14:24). The Lord kept His promise. And when it was time to enter the Promised Land, it was Caleb who flushed the giants out of the mountains. Late into his life, it was still said that he "wholly followed the Lord" (Joshua 14:8-9, 14).

Sadly, many think they can achieve godly goals with divided hearts. When Solomon was old, his wives turned away his heart after other gods so that his heart "was not perfect with the Lord his God, as was the heart of David his father" (1 Kings 11:4). As long as Solomon tried to divide his heart between his wives and the Lord, his devotion faltered. "No servant can serve two masters…" (Luke 16:13). You are either with God all the way, or you are not with Him at all.

Worthless Things

The psalmist vowed, "I will not set before my eyes anything that is worthless" (Psalms 101:3). So much time is wasted on social media. While writing this book I have become convinced that the greatest danger in the online world is the time and mental energy we waste on worthless things. Sure, the hatred, impurity, bullying, and fear of missing out are problems too. But if I had to rank the most dangerous influence on social media, it would be the time we waste on emptiness. Americans spend hours each day looking at a meaningless void that rarely contributes anything toward their spiritual growth and intellectual development. If anything, it subtracts from it. That is why we must keep the psalmist's prayer on the forefront of our minds every day: "Turn my eyes from looking at worthless things; and give me life in your ways" (Psalm 119:37). A "worthless thing" is something that is ineffective, something that in the end amounts to nothing. The prayer is a request for God to take our head in His hands and divert our eyes in another direction away from empty things.[35] We serve a God who will teach us things of weight and value if only we will let Him (Psalm 119:33-40).

Thorny Ground

In the Parable of the Sower, Jesus describes the new convert who loses his focus as "thorny ground": "And as for what fell among the thorns, they are those who hear, but as they go on their way they are choked by the cares and riches and pleasures of life, and their fruit does not mature" (Luke 8:14). He categorizes spiritual distractions in three ways. Some hearts are choked by the "cares" of life. They struggle with worry and allow things that may never happen to have a stranglehold on opportunities that are unfolding now. Some hearts are distracted by the "riches" of life. In Luke 18, a young ruler came to Jesus asking what he needed to do to inherit eternal life. Knowing his heart, Jesus told him that the one thing he lacked was to sell all that he had and distribute to the poor. The young man turned his back on Jesus in sorrow because he was too distracted by his wealth to give his life fully to God (Luke 18:18-23). After he left, Jesus said, "For it is easier for a camel to go through the eye of a needle than for a rich person to enter the kingdom of God" (Luke 18:25). Money makes it harder to follow Christ because it is such a distraction. It takes time to make it, and once you have it, it takes even more effort to hold onto it. That is why the love of money is "a root of all kinds of evils" (1 Timothy 6:10). The final example Jesus gave was the "pleasures of life." Temptation has thrown many Christians off course. Anyone who sins can repent and come back to God, but, sadly, after falling to temptation, many have decided to stay with the devil rather than come back to the Lord. Like thorns, distractions pull at us to draw us away from the Lord. We must weed them from our paths so we do not lose our focus.

Settling for Less

Jesus stopped to rest at the home of some close friends in the little village of Bethany (Luke 10:38-42). One of these friends was Martha, who was "distracted with much serving" (v. 40). We admire her desire to serve. However, she was "distracted." The verb Luke uses literally means "to be pulled or dragged away." Martha's attention was dragged here and there instead of centered upon Jesus.[36] She expected to draw a rebuke from the Lord towards her sister, Mary, with her question: "Lord, do you not care that my sister has left me to serve alone? Tell her then to help me" (v. 40). However, Jesus' reply revealed that there was more to life than work: "Martha, Martha, you are anxious and troubled about many things, but one thing is necessary. Mary has chosen the good portion, which will not be taken away from her." (vv. 41-42). In life, only one thing really matters. Jesus contrasted the two sisters, showing how Martha was "troubled about many things," while Mary chose "the good portion" which could not be taken away from her. We spend so much time on fleeting pursuits, but the good portion lasts forever. You may lose your scholarship, your job, your home, your friends, and even your life, but no one can take away your inheritance in Christ (Romans 8:38-39; 1 Peter 1:3-4).

Was Martha doing anything wrong? Her service was basically good. There is nothing wrong with cooking a meal for somebody and being a good host. Her problem was that she had chosen the good over the best. She allowed herself to be distracted from the most important opportunity she would ever have. In our time, smartphones and social media can be useful tools when we keep them in their place, but too often we allow them to control our attention and pull us away from important opportunities we will never get back again. Jesus shakes us as we stare hypnotically into flashing screens saying, "This is not important! Do not choose this over Me!"

"One Thing"

Jesus has already hinted at the one thing which should be the center of our universe. Other passages also speak of a single-minded focus. Psalm 27:4 reads, "One thing have I asked of the Lord, that will I seek after: that I may dwell in the house of the Lord all the days of my life, to gaze upon the beauty of the Lord and to inquire in his temple." Also, Paul kept his eyes fixed on a solitary focal point: "But one thing I do: forgetting what lies behind and straining forward to what lies ahead, I press on toward the goal for the prize of the upward call of God in Christ Jesus" (Philippians 3:13-14).

Find that "one thing" life is all about and hold onto it with all your might. Jesus told Martha that the "good portion" cannot be taken away from her. You have the power to live a life that matters in Christ. No one and nothing, including social media, can take it away from you. The only threat to your focus is you.

DISCUSSION

1. What distractions might Jesus have faced during His ministry? Do you think it was difficult for Him to keep His focus? What would have happened had He given in and forgotten His purpose?

2. What is the heart's function according to the Bible? Why is it so important?

3. What can happen to an individual who has a divided heart?

4. What is a "worthless thing"? How can we keep our hearts from worthless things?

5. What are the three categories of spiritual distractions Christ gives in the Parable of the Sower?

6. What did Martha do wrong? Was her service bad in itself? How had Mary chosen the "good portion"?

7. What are some questions you can ask to determine what life is really about?

8. Discuss some ways to keep your focus and avoid distractions.

CHAPTER THREE

TIME

On the fourth day of creation, God said, "Let there be lights in the expanse of the heavens to separate the day from the night. And let them be for signs and for seasons, and for days and years" (Genesis 1:14). Moses further explained that these "lights" were "to give light on the earth, to rule over the day and over the night, and to separate the light from the darkness" (vv. 17-18).

The sun, moon, and stars demonstrate the precision with which God created the world. Some believe the world is a great cosmic mishap that happened to turn out pretty well. Their view is about as absurd as betting a horse will win at the races with a billion to one odds just because you like his name.

We are still using this system God put in place for numbering the days and years. Although several systems have been developed for measuring time, astrological data still provide the most reliable standard. For centuries, the orbit of the earth around the sun, as well as the orbital motions of the moon, the stars, and the planets, have been answering the question, "What time is it?"

Time Is Precious
Time must be important, since God invented it. The truth is, time is the very stuff of life. If you ask me for five minutes of my time, you are asking me for five minutes of my life. Time is life, so when you are wasting time, you are wasting life.

And life is valuable. We do not have to be told that. Something within us tells us that life is sacred. One of the strongest human instincts is self-preservation.

The Russian novelist, Fyodor Dostoevsky, was imprisoned for revolutionary activity and brought before a firing squad when he was only twenty-eight years of age. There, standing half naked in the freezing St. Petersburg snow, Dostoevsky thought his short life was over. But at the last moment, as he stood shivering and bewildered, the death sentence was commuted to hard labor in Siberia. Perhaps he was reflecting on that experience when he wrote a scene in his novel, *Crime and Punishment*, in which the main character, Raskolnikov, said,

> Where is it I've read that someone condemned to death says or thinks, an hour before his death, that if he had to live on some high rock, on such a narrow ledge that he had only room to stand, and the ocean, everlasting darkness, everlasting solitude, everlasting tempest around him, if he had to remain standing on a square yard space all his life, a thousand years, eternity, it were better to live so than to die at once! Only to live, to live and live! Life, whatever it may be![37]

What does the Bible say about life? God regards human life so highly that He gave His own Son so that we should not perish but have eternal life (John 3:16). That action tells us life is precious, and it must not be squandered. Jesus asked, "For what will it profit a man if he gains the whole world and forfeits his soul? And what shall a man give in return for his soul?" (Matthew 16:26). The Greek word *psyche*, translated "soul," can also mean "life." Jesus' question leaves us with the impression that no cheap thrill or amount of money is equal to the value of life. Life is precious, and if life is time, time is precious too.

Nine Hours a Day
Are we taking into consideration the value of time when we use social media? The statistics answer this question with an

alarming "No!" Teens are spending nearly nine hours a day online consuming media. For tweens (ages eight to twelve), the average is nearly six hours a day.[38] Now, these figures include streaming TV and listening to music, but 30 percent of this time is spent on social media, two hours per day. That's five years, four months in a lifetime. To put that into perspective, in that same amount of time you could fly to the moon thirty-two times or walk the Great Wall of China three and a half times.[39]

Most of us are not really paying attention to how much time we spend online or doing anything else. We don't want to put a timer on every daily activity, but we must seize control over our schedules. Time is too precious to waste on trivial matters.

Redeeming the Time

"Look carefully then how you walk," Paul writes, "not as unwise but as wise, making the best use of the time, because the days are evil" (Ephesians 5:15-16). The more familiar translation has him urging us to "redeem" the time, but you cannot buy more time, no matter how hard you try. There are only 1,440 minutes in a day, and that is the way it will always be.[40] So "making the best use of the time" is a better translation.

There are two words for "time" in the Greek language. *Chronos* signifies chronological time; it has to do with clocks, calendars, schedules, agendas, and pressure. *Chronos* is not the word used here. The word used here is *kairos*, which has to do with an opportune or appointed time, hence the translation "opportunity" in the NIV.[41] Paul is speaking of using time wisely, of living in what Jerry Sittser calls the "wonder of the present moment."[42] To Paul, the present moment is a wonderful opportunity. "The days are evil"; they soon pass. What a tragedy to waste them!

Poet Philip Larkin asks, "Where can we live but days?" and then remarks that

33

...solving that question
Brings the priest and the doctor
In their long coats
Running over the fields.[43]

Another poet a couple of thousand years removed from Larkin, the Roman emperor, Marcus Aurelius, wrote,

> Even if you are going to live 3000 more years, or ten times that, remember: you cannot lose another life than the one you are living now, or live another than the one you are losing...the present is the same for everyone, and it should be clear that a brief instant is what is lost. For you can't lose the past or the future—how can you lose what you don't possess?[44]

The present is the only time that we really have. We are never in the past or future. Tomorrow never gets here. It is always today. Shouldn't we do our very best with the time that we have?

What Should We Do with Our Time?

Value each moment.
Each day is a gift from God. The Bible reminds us, "This is the day that the Lord has made; let us rejoice and be glad in it" (Psalm 118:24). Life is short; you do not know what a day may bring (Proverbs 27:1; James 4:14).

Does nine hours a day consuming media and ten minutes a day in prayer and study say that we consider time to be a blessing from God? Good stewardship requires us to give back to God a portion of what He has given to us. If we are throwing away all our time on social media, can we say that we are being faithful? It's okay to spend a little time using social media, as long as we do it purposely and keep an eye on the minutes that are passing by. If God has given you time, see it as a blessing, and do not squander it.

Set priorities.
Figure out what's important and spend most of your time on that. Make a list. Ask yourself what's going to make a long-term impact on your life and on the lives of others.

Learn to distinguish between what's "important" and what's "urgent." Most of us think that these two terms mean the same thing, but there is a difference. When you spend time on important matters, you grow and make a little progress toward the big goals you set for your life. Important matters do not happen accidentally. They must be planned. Urgent matters cannot be planned. They are the crises of life, and they must be attended to immediately. Urgent matters can disrupt our lives if we ignore them, but they rarely promote growth or get us any closer to our long-term goals.

Seeking solitude for prayer and meditation is a good example of spending time on something important. Regular time in quiet places with God promotes lasting growth and steadfastness of the soul. It is important, but it is not urgent. In other words, you must look for solitude, it will not look for you. Solitude has to be planned, or it will never happen.

Text messages and the notifications on your phone demand your immediate attention. I'm not even sure if these things should be called "urgent," because most of those digital signals can be ignored without serious consequences. But our phones present an illusion of urgency and, as a result, eat away much of our time. We must resign ourselves, though, to other, more seriously urgent matters. The baby's diaper has to be changed. The phone call you were not expecting has to be answered. The oil has to be changed in the car. Some of your time has to be given to urgent matters. Just don't spend all of your time putting out fires. If you do not spend a significant portion of your time on things that are important, you will never grow. The important matters define success in the long run.

Sometimes we create more crises than necessary because we have neglected the important things. Set aside a little time every day to focus on what is important, and you'll find yourself using the present more for things that you would like to do than for things that you have to do. Pray as Moses instructed: "So teach us to number our days that we may get a heart of wisdom" (Psalm 90:12).

Look for opportunities.
Galatians 6:10 reads, "So then, as we have opportunity, let us do good to everyone, and especially to those who are of the household of faith." Also, James wrote, "So whoever knows the right thing to do and fails to do it, for him it is sin" (James 4:17). The context of this verse is significant. In the verses that precede James 4:17, James talked about the brevity of life and the will of the Lord. The failure he condemned in verse 17, then, is not just about the sin of neglect, but the sin of neglecting the present hour. He is saying, "Whoever knows the right thing to do *now* and fails to do it has sinned."

Opportunities abound in the present, but we fail to see them often because we have our noses stuck in our smartphones. Once you miss an opportunity, you will never get it back again. How many relationships failed because, instead of having a conversation with someone, a person was looking at Facebook? How many good deeds went undone because someone was distracted by Instagram? How many souls have been lost because a Christian did not train himself to be constantly on the lookout for an opportunity to share the gospel? We will never know. One thing is sure: the longer Satan can keep us distracted, the happier he is.

In *The Screwtape Letters*, C.S. Lewis imagines correspondence between two demons, one named Screwtape, and the other Wormwood, on how to mislead people on earth so that they become lost. One of the strategies they discuss is called the "Nothing" strategy. The result of this strategy leaves a person looking back at the end of his life, saying, "I now see that I spent most of my life in doing *neither* what I ought *nor* what I liked." Substitute "day" for "life" and that last statement sounds very similar to what someone might say at the end of a three-hour social media binge. Screwtape explains to his apprentice that the "Nothing" strategy is

> very strong: strong enough to steal away a man's best years not in sweet sins but in a dreary flickering of the mind over it knows not what and knows not why, in the gratification of curiosities so feeble that the man is only half aware of them, in drumming of fingers and kicking of heels, in whistling tunes that he does not like, or in the long, dim labyrinth of reveries that have not even lust or ambition to give them a relish, but which, once chance association has started them, the creature is too weak and fuddled to shake off.[45]

What makes the "Nothing" strategy so effective is that it doesn't have to involve anything explicitly sinful. "I am not doing anything wrong," a person under the spell of this strategy might say. He may be right. But while he is not doing anything wrong, he isn't doing anything right, either.

Is Having Fun a Waste of Time?
Some of you may be reading this and thinking I am arguing that you should delete all your social media accounts, get to work, and never take a break unless it is to catch a few hours of sleep here and there. That is not what I am trying to say. Having fun should be a part of every person's schedule. But what constitutes "fun"

should be *regulated, restorative,* and *righteous* (and, yes, that can include time spent on social media).

In Norman Maclean's *A River Runs Through It,* this is how a father justifies flyfishing to his son:

> As he buttoned his glove in preparation to give us a lesson, he would say, "it is an art that is performed on a four-count rhythm between ten and two o'clock." …I never knew whether he believed God was a mathematician, but he certainly believed God could count and that only by picking up God's rhythms were we able to regain power and beauty.[46]

The father loved flyfishing because something in that leisurely activity helped him regain a sense of "power and beauty." In other words, flyfishing for him had a restorative property and gave him an opportunity to connect with God.

Christians sometimes feel guilty about taking breaks. We are supposed to be responsible, hard-working machines, we think, and not waste our time on useless activities just for the sake of having fun. Where did we get this idea? If work was the most important thing, it would have been one of the Ten Commandments. But look and see if you can find a command to work on the stone tablets. There isn't one, just an assumption that people have to earn a living and that work reflects God's creative nature (Genesis 3:17-19). The only commandment on the subject of work tells us to stop working (Exodus 20:8-11).[47]

Social media can be regulated, restorative, and righteous as long as users are mindful of these three standards as they engage online. *Regulate* your time on social media by setting limits, like thirty minutes a day. Make it *restorative* by using social media to encourage others or seek opportunities to be of service. Ensure that it qualifies as *righteous* by making a covenant with your eyes not to dwell on unwholesome images or words (cf. Job 31:1).

Do I have to become an expert at time management and have enormous to-do lists and be known as a productivity wizard to be pleasing to God? No, God's will for the moment you're in may be to hang out with your friends or eat dinner with your family or sit alone and pray. It may be to assist your neighbor with a need or invite someone to church or share the gospel with a family member. It may be to cook dinner or mow the yard or watch a movie with your brother or sister. It may be to attend Bible class or worship. Paul gave some advice that will help us decide what to do with our time: "…whatever you do, do all to the glory of God" (1 Corinthians 10:31).

Do important, God-driven things with your days. Exchange them like valuable currency, because that's what they are. Your days are either storing up treasure in heaven, or they are spelling a wasted life.

DISCUSSION

1. Who created time? What can we learn from time's origins?

2. What does the Bible say about life? Can you draw a conclusion about time based on what you learned about life?

3. How many hours a day are teens spending consuming media? How much of that time is spent specifically on social media? Do you feel that this is too much time?

4. What does the phrase "redeeming the time" mean?

5. What does Paul mean by the statement, "the days are evil"?

6. What is the only time that we really have?

7. Why should we value our time? How can we do a better job of appreciating each moment as it comes to us?

8. What does it mean to distinguish between the urgent and the important?

9. Why do we miss opportunities? How can we do a better job at seizing the opportunities God gives us?

10. What is the "Nothing" strategy?

11. Do you have to become an expert at time management to please God? What must you do to manage your time in a way that honors the Creator?

CHAPTER FOUR

BOUNDARIES

God takes boundaries seriously. Among the laws that came to Moses on Mount Sinai, we find this isolated regulation: "You shall not move your neighbor's landmark, which the men of old have set, in the inheritance that you will hold in the land that the Lord your God is giving you to possess" (Deuteronomy 19:14). "Your neighbor's landmark" refers to property boundaries. The people of Israel were commanded to respect these borders. Set in antiquity by the "men of old," they were the "ancient landmarks" the wise man reminded his readers about years later (Proverbs 22:28; 23:10). Just because a boundary is old, that does not make it insignificant or irrelevant.

A boundary sets limits. It communicates what is and what is not allowable. A boundary says, "This is mine, and that is yours. You may come to this point, but no farther." A boundary implies that we should not say "yes" to everything and everyone. Some things are not permissible. Some people should be avoided.

Boundaries are helpful in practicing self-control. And when it comes to self-control, we need every advantage. Discipline is hard for everyone, even apostles. Paul said,

> Every athlete exercises self-control in all things. They do it to receive a perishable wreath, but we an imperishable. So I do not run aimlessly; I do not box as one beating the air. But I discipline my body and keep it under control, lest after preaching to others I myself should be disqualified. (1 Corinthians 9:25-27)

Paul is using some interesting language here. "Discipline my body" literally means, "I give myself a black eye." Paul used the image of a boxer in the previous verse and is still borrowing from that imagery as he describes self-control. Boxing gloves in those days were not the fluffy, oversized gloves used in the ring today. They were ox-hide bands covered with knots and nails and loaded with lead and iron.[48] Equally striking is Paul's second description of discipline, "keep it under control," which means, "make my body my slave." The wording pictures a conqueror leading his captives after a battle. Using these two vivid images, Paul reveals how difficult self-control can be. It's like beating yourself in the face with brass knuckles and then chaining yourself up like a slave.

Boundaries make self-control a little easier. They are the decisions that you make before the temptation comes. Say, for instance, you decide that alcohol, for you, is off-limits. When you receive a sudden invitation to a weekend party where there will be drinking, your answer will be ready. You will not have to decide in the heat of the moment what to do. The answer is "no." You know that much because the party lies outside your boundaries.

Free as a (Caged) Bird
M.T. Anderson's novel, *Feed*, pictures a future in which people no longer need computers or smartphones. They access the internet organically through implants in their heads. And what does this continuous feed do for them? They are bored. The story opens with a group of kids who are visiting the moon on spring break. They float in low gravity, listen to live music, go to festivals, ride moon buggies, and play in space, but nothing excites them. "Everything seemed kind of sad and boring," the protagonist, Titus, says. And it's not just the moon. What did he think of Mars? "Mars was dumb."[49] Anderson shows us a future with no boundaries, and the result is boredom. There is nothing

to look forward to, nothing forbidden. Everything is possible, so nothing is possible. Everything is permissible, so nothing is enjoyable.

We live in an age of limitless possibilities. This sounds great until you get frustrated by having to choose from literally millions of possibilities. Music services like iTunes and Spotify provide users with a library of millions of songs, but you can only listen to one at a time. If you are able to settle on something, the whole time you are listening to it you are wondering if you should have chosen something else. This is so different from the days when you had to listen to what was on the radio or select a CD from the limited collection stowed away in your car. Then, it was easier to settle on something and enjoy it. There were limitations, and the limitations enhanced the experience.

In the late 90s and early 2000s, my dad and I traveled to Russia every year to teach in a preacher training school. We stayed in a little flat with no internet access. We were shut off from the outside world in that little space. There was a TV, but we could not understand what anyone was saying on any of the channels. Our only entertainment was a set of six or eight videotapes full of John Wayne movies someone had left behind. We watched every one of those movies. Neither of us was a John Wayne fan back home, but in that flat, John Wayne was our favorite actor. I don't think I could have enjoyed those movies more any place else. The restrictions of that time and place provided me with more possibilities of enjoyment than I would have had with unlimited entertainment.

Poets have known about the usefulness of boundaries for ages. A poet does not have to write a sonnet, a villanelle, or a haiku. He chooses to write in a rhyme scheme or meter because the form channels his mind and sends him to new, creative areas. Ideas sometimes come from the restrictions of the forms as much as they come from the imagination. Even the poetry of the Bible draws from the power of form. Psalm 119 and Jeremiah's lamentations would not have been as effective had the Spirit not imposed acrostics upon the authors' processes.

The truth is, there is no absolute freedom. Seek freedom from God's laws on sexuality, and you will find yourself enslaved to disease, unwanted pregnancies, or heartbreak and shame. Seek freedom from clean living, and you will find yourself enslaved to addiction. Seek freedom from the life of the church, and you will find yourself enslaved to your own spiritual limitations. Paul put it well when he said, "You are slaves of the one you obey" (Romans 6:16). Timothy Keller said, "In many areas of life, freedom is not so much the absence of restrictions as finding the right ones, the liberating restrictions."[50] That's what Jesus told the Pharisees: "You will know the truth, and the truth will set you free" (John 8:32). The truth of the gospel may involve restrictions, but they are the right restrictions that fit with the reality of who we are and the eternity we are destined for.

Boundaries for Social Media

Before you engage with social media, draw a circle around your activities. Decide ahead of time what constitutes a healthy experience online. The boundaries will keep you from making yourself miserable.

Screen time

It is now a well-established fact that excessive amounts of screen use are not good for us. The more time we spend on screens, the less happy and healthy we are. A 2018 study found that children and teens who spend more time on screens scored lower in well-being across eighteen of nineteen different measures.[51] On average, teens are now spending up to nine hours a day on screens, with at least two of those hours engaging in social media. This may have something to do with the problems plaguing kids in America. An unprecedented number are struggling with suicide, depression, and anxiety. They are physically ill. Compared with kids in other parts of the world, Americans ranked almost dead last in physical fitness—forty-seventh out of fifty nations.[52]

Boundaries need to be placed upon how much screen time we allow ourselves every day. The research on well-being points to a limit of about two hours a day, not counting time spent on work. That's enough time for social interaction, entertainment, and games without crowding out other activities that boost physical health, like sleep, face-to-face social interaction, and exercise.[53]

Prepare ahead of your screen time so that you will know where your boundaries are. How much time will you allow yourself to engage with screens during the day? What kind of engagement does this include? Set priorities. Decide what should be done before you allow yourself to get on your smart phone. Also, set a time in the evening, with plenty of time before bed, after which you will not pick up your phone or iPad, except for emergencies. Apple has developed new tools in a recent iOS that will even help you set up notifications to keep yourself in check. The point is, you must make some important choices before engaging with screens if you are going to set any real boundaries.

Privacy

How much will you reveal about yourself online? At best you are engaging with acquaintances, and at worst, complete strangers. Don't give away intimate details of yourself to people who aren't capable of handling your personal information.

God knows you better than you know yourself. Confess and confide in Him. He knows you well enough to handle your deepest secrets. He knows them anyway (Jeremiah 23:24; Psalm 90:8; Matthew 6:8; Hebrews 4:13).

The church should be the place where you reveal your deepest needs and desires. Brothers and sisters in Christ confess their sins to one another and pray for one another so that healing may come (James 5:16). Church is where we keep each other accountable, stir one another up, encourage one another, forgive each other, bear with one another, and love one another (Ephesians 4:32; Colossians 3:13-14; Hebrews 10:24-25). We will develop these ideas more in Chapter 7.

Words

What kind of words do you allow into your heart? What kind of entertainment do you enjoy? What are the themes of the songs you listen to? Are they filled with profanity, sexual innuendo, hatred, and violence? Don't think you can be entertained by a continuous stream of wickedness without being influenced by it. In 2015, researchers from the University of Central Florida examined the relationship between sexual content in music lyrics and the behaviors of young people. Their findings were not surprising. The study showed that "exposure to music containing sexual content is associated with engagement in risky sexual behaviors."[54]

What are you watching? What are you reading? Some of the words we listen to are just empty. They are meaningless because they are materialistic and worldly. Would you absorb those words sitting next to your mom or dad? How would you like it if Jesus were reading over your shoulder, because, in a sense, He is.

What kind of words do you allow out of your mouth? Has social media turned you into a troll? Biblical wisdom teaches, "Whoever belittles his neighbor lacks sense, but a man of understanding remains silent" (Proverbs 11:12). Do you find that your words are harsher online? Is your language coarser when you are typing than it is in face-to-face conversations? Are you thinking before you post?

Think before you speak. Take some time to decide what kind of words will represent you online. Hold yourself to rules like, "No profanity," "Speak with kindness," "What would Jesus say?"

and "Build up, don't tear down." "The heart of the wise makes his speech judicious…" (Proverbs 16:23).

Who Should Draw the Line?

Someone has to make the rules. Who has the authority over our activities on social media? While there may be others who set good boundaries, these three will get you off to a good start.

God

Francis Schaeffer pointed out that Christians have two boundary conditions: (1) what man *can* do, and (2) what man *should* do. The nonbeliever lacks the second boundary. Technology is his only barrier. Schaeffer illustrates with Eve. She had two boundary conditions. She *could* eat the forbidden fruit because it was food and God gave her teeth and a digestive system to eat with. Technology was not her problem. The problem was the fact that God had given a second boundary condition: she *should* not have eaten the fruit of the tree of the knowledge of good and evil, but she did and paid an awful price.[55]

As Christians, we should not just be asking, "What *can* I do on social media?" The additional question should be, "What *should* I do?" As the highest authority, God sets boundaries that are good for us. We would do well to play within them.

Parents

Outside of God, your parents are the best boundary-setters in your life, while you are under their roof. They know you better than anyone does, and they have the benefit of experience, which has taught them wisdom. Good parents share this wisdom with their children in hopes that they can prevent them from making some of the mistakes they made. From the Bible's perspective, a parent who does not discipline his children is harming them. "Discipline your son, for there is hope; do not set your heart on putting him to death" (Proverbs 19:18; cf. Ephesians 6:4).

A house with rules is a happy home. In high school, I remember complaining to a friend about how strict my parents were. He was never supervised and lived his life the way he wanted to. I thought he was pretty happy with the way things were, but he said, "Don't complain about having strict parents. I wish I had a dad who told me what to do. Be thankful." Since then, I have been able to see the good my parents' rules have done in my life. They set boundaries for me before I was able to set them on my own.

You

Boundaries will not do any good unless you decide you are pleased to live within them. If you don't like the rules, it doesn't matter who made them or what the consequences for breaking them will be. Only you can keep you within the proper lines of human behavior. You can put a shock collar on a dog and run electrical wire around the perimeter of your yard, but if he prefers the shock to being cooped up, he will make a run for it. He also may get run over by a car.

Try a "smartphone fast." For one week, no smart phone, internet, or social media. Notice what you can get done without the distractions. Learn how to operate without your digital crutch. Prove to yourself that you can live life off the grid. Like fasting from food, digital fasting is a way of shoring up your spiritual strength. It's discipline for the information age.

For boundaries to work, something has to live within them. One of the reasons people hate rules is they fail to see the good things that can happen while following them. They try not to break the law, but while they're behaving themselves, their lives are like the empty cage at the zoo you were expecting to find full of lions. If we fail to put something within the boundaries, life will be pretty dull. The problem is not with the rules, but with our resistance to life within them. It is not enough to agree upon certain boundaries. Embrace them. Only then will you find the fulfillment and liberation found within the borders.

DISCUSSION

1. What is the purpose of a boundary?

2. How can boundaries aid self-control?

3. How do restrictions make life more fulfilling and enjoyable?

4. What are the effects of excessive screen time upon children and teens?

5. What are some guidelines that could keep you from spending too much time with screens?

6. Why is it important to keep some things secret online? Where can you find a safe environment to confide in others?

7. Do the words we allow into our hearts influence our thinking? What are some good examples?

8. What are some rules you could make to govern your speech online?

9. What are the two "boundary conditions" Christians have?

10. Why should you obey your parents?

11. How might a "smartphone fast" benefit you?

12. Why do we sometimes fail to live successfully within our boundaries?

PART THREE

STARING INTO PHONE-SHAPED POOLS

CHAPTER FIVE

WHO ARE YOU?

"Identity" has to do with the way you see yourself. Your identity is subjective; it is not always accurate, but it is very influential, because much of your feelings and decisions are driven by your answer to the question, "Who am I?"

Social media affects your identity in two ways.

It feels like a tool for reinventing yourself.
We are self-conscious about what we post on social media. The profiles we create are personas, versions of ourselves, not the real person. Sociologist Sherry Turkle quotes one young man who sums this up saying, "Online life is about premeditation."[56] Before we post something, an internal dialogue happens in our head: "Will this make me sound intelligent, or will people think I'm stupid? What kind of an impression will this make? Will this impress my friends or turn them off? Will people think this is funny, or will they not get the joke? How will the online world receive this post?" On social media, we hide the parts of ourselves that we feel are embarrassing. We show the world only the best moments, only the best images. Fragments, not true personalities.

On top of the pressure to seem perfect in the present, social media platforms like Facebook and Twitter archive your posts so that your friends may scroll through months and years of your presentations of yourself. Of course, you can delete them later if you feel they do not project the right image, but even deletions come under scrutiny. In real life, a slip of the tongue or indiscretion might be forgotten in time, but on social media it is preserved for all the world to analyze and dissect. In this regard,

Snapchat, in which posts vanish within moments after they are created, is more like real life, but its illusion of anonymity makes it a dangerous playground.

Building a false persona of yourself on social media treads dangerously close to hypocrisy, a sin Jesus fiercely denounced during His lifetime. He criticized the Pharisees for practicing their righteousness before others to be seen by them. "Woe to you, scribes and Pharisees, hypocrites!" He said, "So you also outwardly appear righteous to others, but within you are full of hypocrisy and lawlessness" (Matthew 6:1; 23:27-28). "Hypocrite" originally had to do with an actor on the stage and naturally evolved to refer to a person who pretends to be someone he or she is not. Is that not what we are doing when we misrepresent ourselves online?

It feels like a weapon that attacks your self-esteem.

While you are creating your own persona, others are doing the same thing on their social media profiles, curating lives to impress their followers. It is easy to scroll through all those idealized versions of your friends and feel that everybody is better than you. Your self-esteem begins to sink every time you open that app on your phone, not because it should, but because you are comparing yourself to false personas created by people also suffering from low self-esteem. Long before the internet, Paul pointed out that comparing yourself to others is not wise (2 Corinthians 10:12). That was when you had to make comparisons from real, personal interactions. Now that we connect through personas instead of real interactions, comparisons are even more foolish.

Our self-esteem crashes not only because of who we think people *are*, but it also takes a hit from what we think people are *doing*. We even have a new word for this affliction: FOMO ("fear of missing out"). We see our friends somewhere having fun, and instead of thinking "Oh! That's nice!" we think, "Why wasn't I invited?" FOMO is nothing more than envy, Shakespeare's green-eyed monster. The feeling is crippling. In the words of the wise man, "Who is able to stand before envy?" (Proverbs 27:4, KJV).

Discovering Your Identity

How we see ourselves comes from one of two opposing systems of self-worth.[57] The world's system of determining self-worth can be summarized by the following equation:

$$\text{Self-Worth} = \text{Performance} + \text{Others' Opinions}$$

According to the world, you are defined by what you achieve or by what people say about you. If we buy into this system, the journey to a positive identity is a climb to a precarious perch. If we are ever able to get there, we can be easily knocked off by one failure or criticism. Unfortunately, the majority of us have accepted this system. As a result, few of us feel worthwhile, and many are trapped in a daily struggle to escape a low self-esteem.

God's system of determining self-worth is very different than the world's:

$$\text{Self-Worth} = \text{God's Declaration about You}$$

According to God's system, you do not have to depend upon your own strength or others' opinions to learn about who you are. Instead, you must turn to God's Word and study what He has declared about you. It goes without saying that this is a far more reliable guide for determining your identity than the world's system, since God has created us and knows us better than we know ourselves (Psalm 139:1-16; Matthew 10:30).

What has God declared? Throughout history, three declarations have dropped like pearls from His mouth.

The first declaration: "You were made in God's image."
Moses writes, "...God created man in his own image, in the image of God he created him; male and female he created them" (Genesis 1:27). This truth is so remarkable, David marveled that God crowned us with "glory and honor" (Psalm 8:3-8). On the sixth day of creation, the Lord made a very different creature, a person unlike any of the animals and plants He had made. The first human being was, in a sense, a child of God. We are not entirely sure what it means to say we have been made in God's image. Maybe it has something to do with self-awareness and the conscience. It almost certainly involves the human soul. Suffice it to say that when God made us, He made something special. So, looking down on us after forming us from the dust of the earth, the Lord declared the human race to be "good" (Genesis 1:31).

The second declaration: "All have sinned."
Everything changed when Adam and Eve made the fateful choice to violate God's commandment and eat the fruit of the forbidden tree in the Garden of Eden. On that day, sin came between the Lord and His beloved human creation. Our ancestors who had been made in God's image were driven away from the garden He had made for them, away from the heart of Eden where the tree of life spread its sap-filled limbs across the abandoned canopy of paradise (Genesis 3:24). Ever since that day, every human being has followed in the footsteps of the first parents and committed sin against the Lord (Romans 3:10, 23; 5:12). If God had stopped with this second declaration, His system of determining self-worth would not be all that helpful to us, but thankfully there is a third declaration.

The third declaration: "Christ died for you."
As with the second declaration, the third declaration has been expressed in a variety of ways throughout Scripture, the most familiar probably being John 3:16: "For God so loved the world,

that he gave his only Son, that whoever believes in him should not perish but have eternal life." Even though humanity turned against God, God did not give up on those who bore His image. Even before they rebelled against Him in sin, God in His majestic foreknowledge determined to save them by sacrificing Himself (1 Peter 1:18-20). When the time was right, God sent His Son to die in our place and redeem us from sin (Galatians 4:4). The apostle Paul summarized it this way in 2 Corinthians 5:21: "For our sake he made him to be sin who knew no sin, so that in him we might become the righteousness of God." Visualize two ledgers. On one is a list of all your sins; on the other, the righteousness of Christ who never sinned. Paul says God has exchanged your ledger for Christ's. Because of His death on the cross, you do not have to answer for your sins. Now when God looks at you, instead of seeing your sin He sees only the righteousness of His Son!

You might try to argue with this third declaration. "But I do not deserve to be made righteous." God says, "I know. I did not say you deserve righteousness. I sacrificed my Son so that you could have His righteousness." To that, you might say, "But can you really do that?" God responds, "Of course I can. I'm God! I can do anything as long as it is consistent with my nature." You persist: "Is it really consistent with your nature to forgive sin?" God could respond, "Yes, my child, as long as my righteousness is satisfied in the cross" (cf. Romans 3:23-26).

The only objection that nullifies God's third declaration about us is, "I don't believe it." Justification comes through faith (Romans 5:1; Ephesians 2:8-9), so not everyone accepts and receives the identity God has made possible for them. Only those who trust in God's promises enough to obey Him can claim this new identity (John 8:24; Luke 13:3; Matthew 10:32-33; Mark 16:16; Acts 2:38; Romans 6:12). This is why the first two declarations apply to every human being, but the third applies only to disciples of Christ. Those who become Christ's disciples no longer allow themselves to be defined by the world. They enjoy the new identity God has given them by grace. "Blessed are those whose lawless deeds are forgiven, and whose sins are covered; Blessed is the man against whom the Lord will not count his sin" (Romans 4:7-8).

Renewing Your Identity

Unfortunately, once you discover your true identity, it is not easy to hold onto it. The world's twisted system keeps creeping back into your mind, threatening the feeling of worth God has given you. That is why you must commit to a daily discipline described in God's Word as "renewal." Paul describes it in Romans 12:2, saying, "Do not be conformed to this world, but be transformed by the renewal of your mind, that by testing you may discern what is the will of God, what is good and acceptable and perfect." Since renewal occurs in the immortal soul, it is possible even as our physical bodies are wearing out. Paul says, "So we do not lose heart. Though our outer self is wasting away, our inner self is being renewed day by day" (2 Corinthians 4:16; cf. Ephesians 4:23; Colossians 3:10). One hearing of God's declaration about you is not enough for it to take root. It takes daily renewal to drive it into your heart so that you will finally come to believe it.

Renew your thoughts about God.
Don't believe the false image about God that says He is against you. God wants you to succeed—truly succeed, according to His definition of success—and He has paid a costly price for our salvation. David said, "For as high as the heavens are above the earth, so great is his steadfast love towards those who fear him" (Psalm 103:11). Jesus is the true image of God. Every day remember Jesus' concern for individuals, compassion for outcasts, and sacrifice for every person. That is God in His true nature (John 1:18; 14:8-10).

Renew your thoughts about your past.

We don't have to forget the past; we just shouldn't let it control us. All of us have made poor decisions and have committed shameful sins (Romans 3:10, 23). But because of Christ, that is no longer who we are. The past has been replaced by the peace of Christ that rules in our hearts (Colossians 3:15).

Renew your thoughts about others.

If we are not careful, we can allow the wounds others have afflicted on us to affect our identity. Blame and bitterness are not good for us. A chance encounter or a post on our newsfeed may trigger a groundswell of hurt feelings. We have a choice: give into the bitterness or forgive. God's Word instructs us to forgive one another as God in Christ has forgiven us (Ephesians 4:32; Colossians 3:12-13).

A common mistake is to think that forgiveness is a one-time action. "I tried to forgive that person years ago," someone might say, "but I still struggle with what he did. I guess it is just not possible for me to forget it." The Bible never says anything about forgiving people the way you flip the light switch. Forgiveness is a process, not a one-time action. You may have to forgive someone several times a day, only to get up in the morning struggling with the same feelings of resentment. Forgive again and again as long as it is necessary (Matthew 18:21-22; Luke 17:3-4).

Renew your environment.

Your struggle with self-esteem may be caused by environmental concerns such as places you go, the people you associate with, or the content you consume online. Don't accept an environment that is bad for you. You have a choice. Look for an environment that provides you with love, harmony, accountability, motivation, and encouragement. While the world offers friendships and places where some of these human needs exist, there is only one place where they are combined: the church (Galatians 6:2; Philippians 2:1-4; James 5:16; Hebrews 10:24-25). The church should be the place we come to find renewal—renewal that beats back the negative messages the world fires at us on a daily basis.

Everyone has days when they feel down and need encouragement. Where is the best place to find strength and renewal? Social media? Not likely. Return to God's proclamations and promises, and they will remind you of who you truly are.

DISCUSSION

1. What is meant by the word "identity"?

2. Do you try to reinvent yourself on social media? What kind of things do you change? What do you try to hide? Do you ever stretch the truth about yourself?

3. How can social media affect your self-esteem? What are some of the things you see on social media that make you feel badly?

4. What is the world's system of determining self-worth?

5. What is God's system of determining self-worth?

6. Which system is more reliable? Why?

7. What are the three declarations God has made?

8. What is God truly like according to the Scriptures?

9. How can we overcome our past?

10. Is forgiveness hard? What are the Bible's requirements with regard to forgiving others?

11. How can your environment affect your self-esteem? How does social media fit into this?

12. What are some daily practices you can develop to renew your mind with God's declarations about you?

CHAPTER SIX

SELFIES

Maybe you've heard the Greek myth of Narcissus, the young man so obsessed with his own image that he drowned looking at it in a pool of water. If our phones were ponds, many of us would have died a long time ago.

When smartphones replaced cameras, we started to face a narcissism epidemic. Suddenly, you no longer had to worry about thirty-five exposures per roll of film, having your camera with you, or wondering whether you were in the frame while taking a picture of yourself. Smartphones solved all those problems. Now, 93 million selfies are taken every day, the equivalent of 2,583,333 rolls of film. One thousand selfies are posted every ten seconds on Instagram, and 75 percent of all posts on Snapchat are selfies. It has gotten so bad that in 2015 more people died from selfies than shark attacks.[58] Millions of photos a day appear on social media of people striking poses, sticking out their tongues, flashing peace signs, and making duck lips, all through a filter that promises to make them look younger and more attractive. It is getting to the point that most of the activity on social media is people taking pictures of themselves for an audience they care nothing about that is doing the exact same thing.

Now, not all selfies are created equally. Who wouldn't want to get in a picture with a celebrity they happened to bump into in New York City? Why wouldn't you occasionally take a picture of yourself having fun with your friends? Most selfies are harmless, but what is this new culture of self-obsession doing to our faith?

The selfie craze would not have impressed Jesus, who said, "If anyone would come after me, let him deny himself and take

63

up his cross and follow me" (Matthew 16:24). The first step of discipleship is dethroning self and crowning Christ in our hearts. He asks us to take up our "cross." Crosses symbolize many things today, but when these words were spoken, they pointed to the ignominy and shame of crucifixion. Jesus is saying, "Follow me, and expect rejection and mockery and perhaps persecution." There are costs to discipleship. This is the idea eloquently expressed by Dietrich Bonhoeffer in the statement, "Every day Christ is [our] death and [our] life."[59]

Paul also promoted self-denial in Romans 12:1-2:

> I appeal to you therefore, brothers, by the mercies of God, to present your bodies as a living sacrifice, holy and acceptable to God, which is your spiritual worship. Do not be conformed to this world, but be transformed by the renewal of your mind, that by testing you may discern what is the will of God, what is good and acceptable and perfect.

Just what is he asking us to sacrifice? First, we must give up our "bodies." This would have raised eyebrows in Paul's original audience, which had been brought up on Plato's teachings. Plato regarded the body as an embarrassing encumbrance. We are not much better. Americans are self-conscious about their bodies. We nearly worship them when we are young and curse them as we get older. But the Bible teaches us that the body is important and that we are to "glorify God" in it (cf. 1 Corinthians 6:19-20). Our bodies will be resurrected and changed at the end of time and ushered into the eternal home they are suited for (1 Corinthians 15:51-53). Perhaps nothing is more inescapable and useful to us than our body. Yet Paul makes an appeal to us based on the mercies of God to *sacrifice* our bodies. This does not mean ritualistic suicide; he is talking about *living* sacrifices. As we walk through life, we must commit our activities to God, whether they be ordinary or remarkable.

He also asks us to sacrifice our "minds." We should think differently than the world. By developing a different attitude, we sacrifice our minds as well as our bodies to Jesus Christ. Paul tells us that our minds are to be transformed by renewal. As we saw in the last chapter, we should use the Word of God daily to renew our minds about God's true nature, about our past, about others, and about ourselves. Every day, our bodies and minds are to be offered up as living sacrifices on the altar of our lives. Christ asks us to give Him our all.

Defending Our Selfies

Believe it or not, self-obsession has been defended since the days of the early church. In 2 Timothy 3:1-5, Paul lists eighteen threats to Christians in the "last days," seven of which concern the problem of selfishness:

> But understand this, that in the last days there will come times of difficulty. For people will be lovers of self, lovers of money, proud, arrogant, abusive, disobedient to their parents, ungrateful, unholy, heartless, unappeasable, slanderous, without self-control, brutal, not loving good, treacherous, reckless, swollen with conceit, lovers of pleasure rather than lovers of God, having the appearance of godliness, but denying its power. Avoid such people.

Notice that at the end of his list, Paul points out that these threats have "the appearance of godliness." The selfishness, along with the other threats to Christian faith, will be defended as good and wholesome. But because these twisted attitudes are impostors, they strip Christianity of its power – they only sound good; they have no spiritual vitality at all.

How do we justify the selfie culture? We defend self-obsession with at least three lies.

"I'm being true to myself."

A few years back, someone criticized Ellen DeGeneres for using her show to promote a homosexual agenda. Her response went viral on Twitter. It was funny, civil, and it sounded reasonable. Here is what she said:

> The only way I'm trying to influence people is to be more kind and compassionate with one another. I don't have an agenda. Attention youth of the world: I want you to live your lives being exactly who you are. Be true to yourself.[60]

What's wrong with that? It's Shakespeare! ("To thine own self be true."[61]) If you are a Christian, this message – "be true to yourself" – creates a problem if "yourself" is different than Christ. Christians are called to sacrifice themselves, not be true to themselves. Paul went so far as to say that his self had been "crucified with Christ" and that it was no longer he who lived but Christ who lived in him (Galatians 2:20).

Some Christians want to make Christianity more palatable by hiding this message. They are unknowingly destroying a fundamental aspect of Christianity. Christ asks us to do something hard. He asks us to deny ourselves, not be true to ourselves, to present our bodies as living sacrifices to God, to allow our minds to be transformed by His Word. This is the difference between the world's agenda and our agenda. The world wants you to be true to yourself; Christ wants you to be true to *God.*

"I'm just telling the truth."

The selfie culture goes beyond social media users taking pictures of themselves. In this fascination with self, there are a lot of comparisons. Harsh comparisons. The kind of faultfinding that slashes and hurts.

When your agenda is to promote yourself, you put yourself in competition with everyone else, which means you have to make others look less attractive, qualified, intelligent, and stylish than you. The unfair criticisms are easy to spot (see Chapter 9). But subtler ones hide behind the banner of truth. The need to put others down feeds a common misunderstanding that if something is true, I have the right to share it. Truth is hijacked as a license to destroy others' reputations. The information you are sharing may be true, but it may not be yours to share. In your zeal to promote yourself, you may become a willing participant in gossip.

Gossip is a serious offense. The wise man said, "Whoever goes about slandering reveals secrets, but he who is trustworthy in spirit keeps a thing covered" (Proverbs 11:13). Before you share information that may hurt another person, ask yourself the following questions:

- *Is it true?* Have you confirmed the truth of what you are about to say? Is your source hearsay? Do everything in your power to ensure the truth of your words.
- *Is it necessary?* Not every fact has to be published. You don't have the right to spread everything you know. The question is, do truth and righteousness demand that I say this?
- *Is it kind?* Our mothers taught us that if we don't have anything nice to say, don't say anything at all. That's good advice.
- *Am I the one to tell it?* The line between gossip and wholesome communication is often drawn by relationships.

If the information you are thinking about sharing passes these four questions, it is not gossip. Just remember, show respect in whatever you share (Romans 12:10; 13:7; 1 Peter 2:17; 3:15).

"If I don't promote myself, no one else will."
Studies have proven that the more time you spend on social media, the more depressed you become. One of the reasons why self-obsession in the cyberworld makes us less content is because we go to our favorite social media site asking, "What's in it for me?" We want those likes and accolades. Meanwhile, the people we're hoping to hear from are wanting the same thing from us. It's just one big unhappy circle.

This discontentment developed online creeps into other areas as well, even church. Instead of walking into a church asking, "What can I do for God?" some of us enter asking, "What can these people do for me?" What would happen if everyone thought this way? Churches would be filled with problems and no solutions. Who would serve? There would be plenty of "needs" but no one to fulfill them. A church filled with self-absorbed, high-maintenance Christians cannot sustain itself. Somebody has to be thinking about others.

Christianity is a "one another" religion. The new commandment Jesus gave to us is to love one another as He loved us (John 13:34-35). We are to consider others more significant than ourselves (Philippians 2:3-4). We cannot be selfish. John asks, "But if anyone has the world's goods and sees his brother in need, yet closes his heart against them, how does God's love abide in him?" (1 John 3:17). Later, he gives this eye-opening truth: "...he who does not love his brother whom he has seen cannot love God whom he has not seen" (1 John 4:20).

Of course, selfish discontent has been around a lot longer than the internet. Social media has just launched it into overdrive with its obsession with self. We don't even see anything wrong with it anymore. The entire world is staring at its own image, and that image is being projected in the shiny glass screen of a smartphone.

Correcting Our Selfies

People like to use filters to make their selfies look better. The jury is still out on whether tweaking your image is fooling anybody. Before this chapter ends, we will discuss some corrections that need to be made to our images, but we will not be talking about photographs. These corrections have to do with the moral shortcomings of self-obsession.

Don't be insecure.

Selfishness makes us insecure. We fear others' successes, running out of praise, rejection, and loneliness. We are afraid, so we gobble up whatever validation we can find and give nothing away. We become junkies, feeding off the empty calories of an online praise factory.

Christ was never insecure. He made the world better through sacrifice. Sacrifice is the opposite of insecurity. Jesus gave courageously because He knew the secret of generosity – that generosity and love for others will never deplete your value. They are like the oil of the widow of Zarephath (1 Kings 17:8-16). They never run out. Thomas Jefferson said, "A candle loses nothing when it lights another candle." Those who focus on themselves are discontent and constantly feel needy, but those who concentrate on helping others find their need for self-worth constantly in full supply (cf. 2 Corinthians 9:6).

Don't make an idol of yourself.

An idol is anything you put before God. Because self-centeredness puts something before God—yourself—it is idolatry. Flannery O'Connor once expressed this hard truth, praying: "I do not know you God because I am in the way."[62] Idols make life about the wrong thing. We cannot be happy or fulfilled

69

when we put anything, including ourselves, before the Lord (cf. Ecclesiastes 12:13; Matthew 6:33).

Beware of pride.
If you don't think pride is dangerous, remember that it was pride that created the devil, pride that created hell (1 Timothy 3:6). Pride...

- Hardens the mind (Daniel 5:20).
- Produces spiritual decay (Hosea 7:9-10).
- Keeps real progress from happening (Proverbs 26:12).
- Keeps us from coming to God (Psalm 10:4).
- Leads to destruction (Proverbs 16:18).

When you are proud, you are either a bully or a baby. Bullies push people around, taking a "my way or the highway" mentality. Babies whine about what they don't have, and pout over others' triumphs.[63]

Develop empathy.
When you care only for yourself, you are apathetic toward others. People become objects to use for your own purposes. You lose a sense of how they feel, and the apathy gets worse in the virtual world in which everything is mediated through a screen. We forget real people are on the receiving end of our posts and criticisms. They see the fun we are having and feel envious; they read our opinions and feel defensive; they see our selfies and react accordingly.

Even though He was God, Christ could feel others' pain and joy. He shared in their sorrows and celebrated their triumphs. He sang with them and prayed with them. In Christ we have a high priest who can sympathize with our weaknesses (Hebrews 4:15). We must follow His lead by encouraging the fainthearted, helping the weak, and being patient with all (1 Thessalonians 5:14).

Before you snap that next selfie, ask yourself, "Why do I feel the need to post another picture of my face?" Are you looking for someone's approval? Are you deeply insecure? Or are you just excited about a trip that you took or someone you met? Not all selfies are bad, but selfishness is sin.

Maybe it would be helpful to scroll through a few selfies of others and do a gut check on your reactions to their pictures. Do you enjoy looking at digital self-portraits? Do they make you feel jealous? Do you think others feel differently than you when they see your pictures?

The world is becoming more and more self-obsessed. We may not know where this self-centeredness might lead, but we can be sure that it is leading us farther away from Christ. Pictures say virtually nothing about who you are, but the throne room of your heart reveals everything. Who rules within? The answer to this question matters so much more than pixels on a screen.

DISCUSSION

1. What did Jesus mean when He said we should take up our cross and follow Him? (Matthew 16:24).

2. What does Paul tell us to sacrifice in Romans 12:1-2?

3. Read 2 Timothy 3:1-5. Can you find the seven threats that relate to selfishness?

4. What's wrong with the advice, "Be true to yourself"?

5. How does the selfie culture lend itself to comparisons? Are these comparisons healthy?

6. What's wrong with gossip? What are four questions you should ask before sharing information that will help you make sure you are not about to spread gossip?

7. What's wrong with asking, "What's in it for me?" when looking for a church?

8. What kind of fears are fostered by selfishness?

9. What is an idol? Who do we worship when we become self-obsessed?

10. Why is pride dangerous? What can we do to keep our pride in check?

11. What is empathy and how can we develop it?

CHAPTER SEVEN

PROFILES

Evolutionary science collides with the Bible in a number of ways, not least in the idea that all life came from nonliving matter and that there is little difference between humans and animals. It is argued that we may be more highly developed, but we are still just beasts, hairless apes with large frontal cortexes. The Bible, on the other hand, argues that only humans have been made in God's image. Dominion over the world has been given to them, and they have been tasked to "be fruitful and multiply and fill the earth and subdue it" (Genesis 1:28).

The Bible works from this premise when it suggests in Romans 12:3 that there is a way humans "ought" to think of themselves: "For by the grace given to me I say to everyone among you not to think of himself more highly than he ought to think, but to think with sober judgment, each according to the measure of faith that God has assigned." The emphasis here is upon not being arrogant, not thinking "more highly" of yourself. But if there is a way that we "ought" to think, it is just as possible to think too lowly of yourself.

So while we must be careful about making ourselves appear better than we are on social media, we must also take care not to make ourselves appear worse. Wisdom suggests that we should scroll through our photos, likes, links, and posts from time to time, asking ourselves, "Is there anything shameful or embarrassing on here? Does my profile have the potential of ruining an opportunity for me in the future?"

It happens all the time. Employers often look at the social media accounts of the applicants they are considering for a job. On the basis of nothing more than their social media profile, some applicants are tossed out before they even get to the interview. Profiling like this happens on college campuses too. A survey conducted by Kaplan Test Prep found that admissions officials at more than two-thirds of colleges say it's "fair game" for them to review applicants' social media profiles on sites like Facebook, Instagram, and Twitter to help them decide who gets in.[64] A bad profile can even ruin a person's chance for a long-term, fulfilling relationship. How would you feel if you learned that you were turned down for a date because the person you liked saw something questionable on your Facebook account?

"That's not fair," you might say. "My profile is not the real me!" You're right. It is impossible to know somebody fully by merely browsing through his social media accounts. But in a world that has been using this technology for almost two decades, we have to cope with potential employers, admissions officials, and friends who have come to rely on fragments as representations of the entire person. Don't be naïve. People are making judgments about you from your online persona.

We have already addressed hypocrisy. It is wrong to pretend to be someone you are not. But that does not mean you have to reveal everything about yourself to the world. In fact, Scripture gives three important directions regarding public image that should guide your use of social media.

Protect Your Good Name

"A good name is to be chosen rather than great riches, and favor is better than silver or gold" (Proverbs 22:1). "Name," as it is used here, has to do with your reputation or how people have come to regard you. Some take a good name and ruin it. "Jezebel" might once have been a pretty name, but after Ahab's evil queen was finished with it, it became a name no mother would dare to give her child. On the other hand, "Caleb" originally meant "dog." But during the days of Joshua, a man with that name conquered giants for God despite his humble beginnings. He made his name great.

Protecting your good name may benefit your future prospects, but there is an even more important reason to preserve your reputation. As Christians, we must remember that we represent God. Ruining our name puts a stain on the body of Christ. Concerned with this problem, the apostle Peter wrote to a group of Christians suffering from persecution, saying, "Keep your conduct among the Gentiles honorable, so that when they speak against you as evildoers, they may see your good deeds and glorify God on the day of visitation" (1 Peter 2:12). His logic is sound. You cannot control what others say, but you can control the credibility of their words. If your conduct remains honorable, people will not believe their slander very long. Eventually their lies will be exposed by the light of your character. Peter recognized that there are times a person deserves his suffering. If his brothers and sisters had to suffer, Peter's prayer was that their pain would be an injustice, not a result of crime, so that they would not be ashamed but glorify God as Christians (1 Peter 4:15-16).

Don't Weary the World

In one of the more humorous proverbs of Solomon, the wise man gives some good relationship advice: "If you have found honey, eat only enough for you, lest you have your fill of it and vomit it. Let your foot be seldom in your neighbor's house, lest he have his fill of you and hate you" (Proverbs 25:16-17). What happens when you eat too much candy? You get sick. There is such a thing as too much of a good thing. Solomon compares the kid who ate too much candy to a neighbor who is growing weary of a friend's constant presence. Essentially what he is saying is this: *don't wear out your welcome*. Visit just enough to leave your neighbors wanting more.

The same rule applies to social media. We have all grown weary of the friend who seems to be constantly online. We have all had the experience of opening up Facebook to discover that our news feed has been besieged by one person's late-night sharing binge. We get on to look at pictures of family and friends, but all we see are those annoying placards and pictures of food we cannot eat. We have all seen those bewildering announcements about mundane, every day experiences ("I'm up!" "Coffee, now!") All of us know the feeling of being the victims of what I heard somewhere called the "Chinese water-drip of Facebook status messages."

There are numerous reasons why someone might overuse social media in these ways. Sharing brief, nearly meaningless messages throughout the day can give friends who follow your updates a sense of the rhythm of your life. Sociologists call it "ambient awareness." It's almost like being in the same room as someone and picking up on his mood and thoughts by the signals he is giving off.[65] It works with friends who take a personal interest in the trickle of those mundane posts, but how many lives can any one of us care about down to the details of what someone had for dinner and what TV program she is about to watch? If you are sharing a lot of details, be careful; you could be wearing out your welcome.

Oversharing could be a desire to give your followers a feel for the rhythm of your life, or it could just be a symptom of self-centeredness. Thinking people might actually be interested in the smallest details of their lives, some people post meaningless messages like addicts who cannot control their fingers. Meanwhile, their friends are starting to get sick of the honey.

The internet has given us a dangerous feeling of self-importance. Anybody can post anything online. And most of us do it expecting other people to read with rapt interest.

Christianity, however, is meant to focus on others. Consider these passages:

- "Everyone who exalts himself will be humbled, and he who humbles himself will be exalted" (Luke 14:11).
- "Outdo one another in showing honor" (Romans 12:10).
- "Love does not envy or boast" (1 Corinthians 13:5).
- "[Submit] to one another out of reverence for Christ" (Ephesians 5:21).
- "In humility count others more significant than yourselves" (Philippians 2:3).

We're not here for ourselves. We're here to make others' lives more valuable.

Ironically, when you puff yourself up using social media, or in the old-fashioned way, you feel miserable. It's focusing on others that makes you truly happy. God didn't wire us to be self-centered. We were made to serve.

The best way to control an overabundance of posts is to unplug for a while and gain some perspective in the real world. But even while you are online, you can be more conscious of others, following the Bible's guidance on listening and considering others to be more important than you (James 1:19; Philippians 2:3-4).

Keep Some Secrets

Not everything needs to be told. "He lives well who hides well," to quote the Roman poet Ovid. We talk a lot about the Christian's responsibility to reveal secrets, confessing our sins to one another so that we may pray for one another (James 5:16), but we do not think much about *keeping* secrets.

The book of Proverbs has a lot to say about those who share others' secrets. Gossip is tempting because there are always willing ears to consume it. "The words of a whisperer are like delicious morsels; they go down into the inner parts of the body" (Proverbs 26:22). But we must resist the temptation to share things we have no right to share. Revealing another's personal information is slander and strife (Proverbs 11:13; 20:19; 25:9). If you love someone, you will protect their secrets. By withholding information, you strengthen your relationships by building trust.[66]

We do not like it when others share our secrets, which makes it hard to understand why we are so quick to share our own on social media. Secrets are an important way of holding onto your dignity. Wendy Shalit explains: "Our dignity is in our secrets. If nothing is secret, nothing is sacred."[67] In other words, people who are not close to you are not prepared to know you fully. If you share certain personal information with them before they are ready, the result is shame. Your privacy is exchanged for their entertainment or manipulation. With no secrets to guard you from their scrutiny, you get buried in humiliation.

Samson had lots of secrets, but he chose poor confidants. First, having killed a lion with his bare hands, he later found honey in the carcass and ate some of it. This became the basis for the unsolvable riddle he told at his wedding feast: "Out of the eater came something to eat. Out of the strong came something sweet." His companions had seven days to solve the riddle, or they would have to cough up thirty linen garments and thirty changes of clothes. Not knowing the answer to the riddle, they pressured Samson's new wife to entice him to reveal the answer, which she did. When they discovered Samson's secret, they embarrassed him by answering his riddle in front of everybody on the seventh day of the feast. Samson reacted by killing thirty men and returning to his father's house in hot anger. Meanwhile, his wife was given to his best man (Judges 14:1-20). The second instance also involved a woman, a Philistine named Delilah. Samson was a Nazirite. A razor had never touched his head. As long as he kept his seven long locks, God would endow him with amazing strength. The Philistines wanted to know the source of Samson's strength and offered Delilah 1,100 pieces of silver in exchange for the secret. After several attempts, she finally wore him down. Samson revealed his deepest secret to someone who did not really love him, and the shame was worse than even before: his enemies gouged out his eyes while Delilah tormented him, and he was forced to grind mill in a Philistine prison while his enemies mocked him for entertainment (Judges 16:1-27).

A Safe Place for Intimacy

"Intimacy" is a state of being in which you are known and loved.[68] We all desire intimacy. That's part of being human. But intimacy with people who cannot be trusted is dangerous. You take a big risk by revealing your life to others. After learning your secrets, will they still love you? Maybe not. There is no shortcut to safe intimacy. If you reveal too much of yourself too soon, as we are tempted to do online, you risk putting your most personal secrets, the mystery of you, in the hands of someone who may abuse that information.

Your need for privacy is determined by intimacy. The less you know someone, the less they have a right to know about you.

At the top of the list, God knows us better than we know ourselves. "Can a man hide himself in secret places so that I cannot see him?" He asks, "Do I not fill heaven and earth?" (Jeremiah 23:24). Hebrews 4:13 says, "And no creature is hidden from his sight, but all are naked and exposed to the eyes of him to whom we must give account." There is no use trying to hide from God. Not only does He know us, but a relationship with Him is our only hope for salvation. Attempts to move away from Him are signs that something is amiss in our spiritual lives. Consider Adam and Eve. At first, they were very much at home with God in the garden, but after they sinned, they hid themselves from the presence of the Lord (Genesis 3:8). God drove them even farther from His presence, barring them from the garden of Eden and the tree of life, a sign of their spiritual desolation.

Through Christ, we have hope of reconciliation, which is a return to spiritual intimacy with God (2 Corinthians 5:18-20; Colossians 1:20). To be known by Him fully, with the bright light of His righteousness shining upon all our sins and weaknesses, and yet still loved by Him, is perhaps the greatest mystery of all. Who can be known and loved by God and not fall down in worship to Him?

As God's children, we confess our sins and share our innermost thoughts with Him in prayer, yet we still feel the need to express these private concerns to others. This is why so much content gets uploaded to the internet that should not be there. Surely, there is a safer place to reveal our true selves.

God has created a safe place where we can be known and loved among others in the church. In the New Testament, the church was a place in which people had all things in common (Acts 2:44), suffered together and rejoiced together (1 Corinthians 12:26), confessed their sins to one another (James 5:16), held each other accountable (Matthew 18:15-18; 1 Corinthians 5:1-2), confronted one another (Galatians 2:11), and encouraged one another (Hebrews 10:25). They got into one another's business. Things got personal. These days, we don't like for people to learn too much about our lives. We change the subject when the conversation gets deep, or we get nervous when a stranger unexpectedly reveals that he knows something about us. But in the ancient world there was no such thing as a private life.[69] This may have created problems in other areas, but sharing personal matters was safe in the church. What made it safe was the intimacy. The church wasn't just an organization, it was a family – brothers and sisters in the body of Christ.

Because of love, the church should be the safest place on earth to show your true colors. Your brothers and sisters should embrace and forgive you, even when they know you, warts and all. The result of this intimacy is a deep sense of belonging, a sense that you matter to others, as well as to God.

Outside of those who know us best—our churches, our families, our spouses, and our closest friends—we should filter our personal information so that nothing gets into the hands of people who might try to use it to harm us. This is not easy. Even when we put forth our best efforts, we can become victims of identity theft, unfair judgments, or voyeurism. We don't have to give ourselves away, though. With a little wisdom we can maintain our dignity.

What are we to make of those who seem to want to know more about us than they have a right to? One of my favorite movies is *Rear Window* (1954), directed by Alfred Hitchcock. James Stewart plays a photographer who is recovering from a broken leg and confined to his apartment in Greenwich Village. Through his apartment window, he is able to observe his neighbors carrying out their personal lives. He even uses his zoom lens to get a closer look. Most of the time, he doesn't witness anything interesting, just people bringing home groceries, practicing the piano, talking on the telephone, or having an argument. But one night he thinks he sees a murder. Does he intervene? How does he explain to the police how he came by this information? What will the authorities think about a man who spends his evenings staring at his neighbors without their permission?

Sometimes having a social media account feels like you are being stared at by a creep looking at you from his apartment's rear window. Keep in mind that the strong desire we see on social media for personal knowledge is really a desire for love. There are a lot of lonely people in the world who need real, committed relationships. Our work as Jesus' disciples is to offer them a chance to be fully known and loved. But there are no shortcuts. Christ paid an awful price so that we might have the chance to be one body in Him. Anybody can have this true intimacy, but not without first denying himself, taking up his cross, and following the Savior (Matthew 16:24).

God already fully knows each one of us. Despite our flaws, He calls us to a life with Him through the reconciliation of the cross. We may acknowledge our secrets before Him now, or we can pretend He doesn't know them. But one day, all of us will stand before Him at judgment, and everything will be revealed – good and bad (Ecclesiastes 12:14; Romans 2:16; 2 Corinthians 5:10).

DISCUSSION

1. How could a social media profile ruin an opportunity for you in the future?

2. What is a "good name"? Can a person ruin a good name? Can a person make a bad name great?

3. What are some reasons why we should protect our good name?

4. What does it mean to "wear out your welcome" on social media?

5. Why might people overuse social media?

6. Where should the focus of Christians be?

7. What is the best way to get control over an overabundance of social media posts?

8. What's wrong with gossip? What does it do to relationships?

9. How are secrets connected to dignity?

10. What happened to Samson when he told his secrets?

11. To whom should we entrust our secrets?

12. How do we cope with knowing that God will judge us, including our secrets, on the last day?

PART FOUR

I WANT TO SEE YOU NOT THROUGH THE MACHINE

CHAPTER EIGHT

FRIENDS

Maybe the most dangerous deceit on social media is Facebook's use of the word "friend." Twitter and Instagram have "followers," but Facebook calls the people you connect with "friends." This language may seem innocent, but it is changing our understanding of what a true relationship is. It is possible to have thousands of "friends" on Facebook and be extremely lonely. Social media began as a way to connect, but despite its constant presence for nearly two decades, we are more disconnected than ever.

We are getting closer to the future E.M. Forster predicted in his eerie dystopian novel, *The Machine Stops*. The novel describes the relationship between a mother, Vashti, and her son, Kuno. Life on the surface of the earth has become uninhabitable, so what's left of humanity lives in cavities underground, each person isolated to his or her own room. Every need required to sustain this disconnected existence is supplied by the Machine, a mysterious, seemingly omnipotent device invented by humanity before a time anyone can remember. Kuno has not seen his mother in a long time, although they frequently chat through the Machine, which keeps the population connected at all times (sound familiar?). That is not enough for Kuno. He messages his mother to ask her if she would visit him. "I want you to come and see me," he says. "But I can see you!" she protests, "what more do you want?" "I want to see you not through the Machine," he says. The son knew something most of the human race had forgotten – that there is a difference between long-distance messages and face-to-face relationships.[70]

In her article for *The Atlantic*, Jean Twenge interviews a 13-year-old girl who says, "I think we like our phones more than we like actual people." Wise beyond her years, the young girl has made a distinction few of her peers have yet to recognize. Merely connecting to someone on a phone or an iPad is not the same thing as a relationship. In one case, you are relating to a device. In the other, you are relating to a person.

Twenge's research demonstrates that the arrival of the smartphone has changed every aspect of teenagers' lives. They are going out less, less likely to date, and are getting their driver's license later in life. The number of teens who get together with their friends nearly every day dropped by more than 40 percent from 2000 to 2015. Teens today are not working as much. They are taking fewer risks. They are safer, but only because they are not out in the world where the dangers are. Adulthood waits longer for iGen teens. Because they choose to stay in their rooms instead of mingling with others in the world, childhood now stretches into high school.[71] Journalist Nancy Jo Sales wrote about a conversation she had with one young person who said, "Social media is destroying our lives." "So why don't you go offline?" Sales asked. The young girl said, "Because then we would have no life."[72] Social media feels like a trap – if you jump in, you enter an environment of connections that cannot replace real-life relationships, but if you jump out, you feel disconnected.

Don't let its name deceive you. Social media is gradually taking away our social skills. People are getting less comfortable with personal interaction, eye contact, and spontaneous conversation. In Isaac Asimov's prescient 1957 novel, *The Naked Sun,* a police detective named Baley investigates a murder on the planet Solaria, where individuals live alone in enormous estates having very little contact with others except through technology. Baley, an earthman who prefers face-to-face contact, makes everyone uncomfortable, demanding to meet with each of his suspects personally. The discomfort this causes the inhabitants of

Solaria is evident in a face-to-face exchange between Baley and Quemot, a sociologist. "It has been a long time since I've done anything like this," says a nervous Quemot. The sociologist turns sharply from his guest and retreats to a chair at the opposite end of the room, angling it so that it faces more away from the detective than toward him and sits down. His hands are clasped and his nostrils quiver. It takes every fiber of his being to keep from leaping from his chair and running away.[73] Hopefully, our ability to socialize will not degenerate to the level of the Solarians. One thing is sure, social media is pushing us closer to Asimov's dystopian future, not moving us away from it.

Relationships, Who Needs Them?

Who needs relationships anyway? Human interaction is awkward, risky, messy, and sometimes painful. Everyone knows what it's like to have been betrayed by a friend. Two people can be best friends one year and mortal enemies the next. Men have a particularly tough time building meaningful, safe relationships. Only two out of ten men say they have friends they can trust. On the other hand, six out of ten women say they have friends that can rely on.[74] Even marriage, the closest human relationship on earth, breaks down on a regular basis. On any given year in the U.S., between 40 to 50 percent of marriages end in divorce.[75] There are some encouraging signs that divorce may be on the decline, but one theory says this trend is the result of fewer marriages. Even Jesus was betrayed with a kiss by one of his hand-picked disciples, reminding John of David's psalm: "Even my close friend in whom I trusted, who ate my bread, has lifted his heel against me" (Psalm 41:9; John 13:18). Relationships are hard. People get hurt. Are they worth the trouble?

We are tempted to retreat to the safe environment of social media, where we have time to think before we reply and choose our words carefully, but we must brave the real world of human interaction. Friendships are important. Since the beginning of time, God has declared, "It is not good that the man should be alone" (Genesis 2:18). Proverbs 17:17 says, "A friend loves at all times, and a brother is born for adversity." In other words, a friend is one of the few things in the world you can count on.

Friendship has been scientifically proven to improve the quality of one's life. Dr. James J. Lynch shows in his book, *The Broken Heart*, that lonely people live significantly shorter lives than the general population. Also, studies at the Carnegie Institute of Technology reveal that even in a field like Engineering, about 15 percent of a person's financial success is due to his or her technical knowledge, and about 85 percent is due to skill in human engineering—the ability to make friends and deal with people personally. Dr. William Menninger has found that when people are fired from their jobs, "social incompetence" (the inability to interact with others) accounts for 60 to 80 percent of the failures.[76]

Friendship is invaluable because it makes even the most insignificant people special. Robert Louis Stephenson wrote, "So long as we are loved by others, I would almost say that we are indispensable; and no man is useless while he has a friend." Henry David Thoreau sometimes awoke in the night to think of "friendship and its possibilities."[77] Just think about all the characters in the Bible who were made great with the help of their friends. Where would Ruth have been without her mother-in-law, Naomi? Where would David have been without his best friend, Jonathan? What would Paul have done without Barnabas, Silas, and Timothy?

We want to spend our lives on valuable things, things that matter. God's Word says that one of the most valuable treasures on earth is the human soul (Genesis 1:26-27; Psalm 8:3-5; Matthew 16:26). Friendship, by definition, is the knitting together of souls (Deuteronomy 13:6; 1 Samuel 18:1). Why would we not want to attach ourselves to something so valuable as another's soul?

How to Make Real Friends

It is easy to accept a friend request on Facebook. It is much harder to make a true friend in the real world. Relationships are hard. Friendship is rare. Henry Adams said, "One friend in a lifetime is much; two are many; three are hardly possible." Because there are so many variables in the unpredictable dynamic of human relationships, it is impossible to give guarantees for making friends, but biblical wisdom does provide some helpful advice.

Get interested in others.

Dale Carnegie said, "You can make more friends in two months by becoming interested in other people than you can in two years of trying to get other people interested in you." Social media is a self-centered place. You go online to post about yourself and to see who "likes" you, and that is why it's so bad at fostering true relationships. You will never make a friend if you are thinking only of yourself. It's cliché, but to have friends, you must *be a friend.* Andrew Sullivan calls this "reciprocity" and writes,

> Unlike a variety of other relationships, friendship requires an acknowledgement by both parties that they are involved or it fails to exist. One can admire someone who is completely unaware of our admiration, and the integrity of that admiration is not lost; one may even employ someone without knowing who it is specifically one employs; one may be related to a great-aunt whom one has never met (and may fail ever to meet). And one may, of course, fall in love with someone without the beloved being aware of it or reciprocating the love at all. And in all these cases, the relationships are still what they are, whatever the attitude of the other person in them: they are relationships of admiration, business, family, or love.

But friendship is different. Friendship uniquely requires mutual self-knowledge and will. It takes two competent, willing people to be friends. You cannot impose a friendship on someone, although you can impose a crush, a lawsuit, or an obsession. If friendship is not reciprocated, it simply ceases to exist or, rather, it never existed in the first place.[78]

Friendship is unique among relationships in its requirement of mutual interest. Wanting to shield the fractured relationships at Philippi, Paul wrote, "Do nothing from selfish ambition or conceit, but in humility count others more significant than yourselves. Let each of you look not only to his own interests, but also to the interests of others" (Philippians 2:3-4).

Don't worry about popularity.
Victor Hugo called popularity "glory's small change." Social media puts us in a competition to see who can get the most followers, as if that has something to do with happiness or love. Right now, Katy Perry leads the pack on Twitter with more than 106 million followers. Most of those followers know nothing about Katy. She may be popular, but that does not mean she has fulfilling relationships in her life.

Don't expect to be included in everything. You are going to scroll through your newsfeed and see people enjoying themselves. The ability to instantly share videos and pictures of outings while we are engaged in them has opened up a whole new world of feeling left out. You have probably felt this way before. You're home and bored, so you scroll through your newsfeed only to see people you thought were your friends having a good time without you. Don't cave to fear of missing out. Jealousy is a turnoff. Who knows why you weren't included? Odds are, your friends planned that activity you missed out on while you happened to be away from them. Most of the time, the reasons why we are left out are innocent. Remember that the goal is not to be the most popular person in the world or attend every exciting social function. The goal is to have healthy, fulfilling relationships in your life.

Proverbs 18:24 warns, "A man of many companions may come to ruin, but there is a friend who sticks closer than a brother." You have to make too many compromises to become popular. Also, it is impossible to be close to hundreds of so-called friends at a time. The goal should be to have a few friends you can count on, friends who stick "closer than a brother."

The Greek language is better equipped to measure the quality of relationships than English, which has only "love" to describe innumerable degrees of intimacy. The Greeks had at least four terms to describe love:

- *Storge* is fondness for those who are naturally close to you, like the feeling a mother has for her child.
- *Eros* is a word for romantic love. *Eros* was also the Greek name for the mythological god, Cupid, whose arrows, once they struck their target, filled the intended with uncontrollable desire.
- *Philia* represents warm, affectionate love, the love of friends. In the Bible, it is combined with the Greek word for "brother" to denote *philadelphia,* "brotherly affection" (cf. 2 Peter 1:7).
- *Agape* signifies the truest and purest form of love that we learn from God (1 John 4:7-10).

Whether or not we have the words to measure it, the quality of our relationships matters so much more than the quantity. A few true friends are to be desired more than thousands of fair-weather acquaintances.

Don't pursue friends, pursue a purpose.

A person's first inclination about making friends might be to look for someone interesting and attempt to force a friendship into being. As strange as it sounds, this approach does more harm than good. No one likes for someone to have friends pushed on them. Furthermore, what does resorting to pleading, pleasing, groveling, and smothering do to you? You may gain a few companions, but at what cost? What happens to your values while you are trying to attract the in-crowd? In his book *The Four Loves*, C.S. Lewis discusses the pitfall of pursuing friends:

> That is why those pathetic people who simply "want friends" can never make any. The very condition of having Friends is that we should want something else besides Friends. Where the truthful answer to the question Do you see the same truth? would be "I see nothing and I don't care about the truth; I only want a Friend," no Friendship can arise—though Affection of course may. There would be nothing for the Friendship to be about; and Friendship must be about something, even if it were only an enthusiasm for dominoes or white mice. Those who have nothing can share nothing; those who are going nowhere can have no fellow-travellers.[79]

Think about it: how did you meet your best friend? Did you become friends because one of you chased the other? Or did you meet one another while engaged in something you really cared about? If you want true friends, find a purpose, and go for it. It should be added that the quality of the purpose you pursue has a bearing on the quality of the friends you make. If you are not around the right crowd, change your pursuits, and you will make new relationships that will be better for you.

Even Jesus needed friends. He often found respite in the home of Lazarus, Martha, and Mary (John 11:5). He chose the twelve apostles "that they might be with him and he might send them out to preach" (Mark 3:14). Within those twelve, Jesus selected an "inner circle" of three: Peter, James, and John (Mark 5:37; 9:2; 14:33). Because He was human, Jesus needed friends.

Jesus has also invited *us* to be His friends! "You are my friends," He says, "if you do what I command you" (John 15:14). And what has He commanded us? "This is my commandment, that you love one another as I have loved you" (John 15:12). As long as we enter into a covenant relationship with Christ and reflect the love of God to one another, we can claim Jesus as a friend! But many of us treat Him as if He were a Facebook friend. We "like" Him, check in on Him from time to time, scroll through His Word for interesting posts, and we may even message Him from time to time. But do we take risks to really *know* Him? The apostle Paul was willing to give everything up for this privilege: "Indeed, I count everything as loss because of the surpassing worth of knowing Christ Jesus my Lord. For his sake I have suffered the loss of all things and count them as rubbish, in order that I may gain Christ" (Philippians 3:8).

All over the world, people are being crushed by loneliness. But social media is not the solution to our relationships. In fact, it only exacerbates the problem. To have true relationships, we have got to get out into the world where interactions are awkward, messy, and often fraught with missteps and misunderstandings. We have to risk betrayal. We might get hurt. But the risks are worth the rewards because in a friend we stand to gain a connection to one of the most precious things on earth—a human soul.

DISCUSSION

1. What is the difference between a Facebook friend and a real-life friend?

2. Has social media made us more social or less?

3. Why are we tempted sometimes to replace real-life human interaction with social media?

4. Are friendships important? Why should we risk the messy world of human interaction?

5. What is a friend?

6. How is social media a self-centered place?

7. What are some ways you can show interest in other people and take the focus off of yourself?

8. Is popularity important? What is more important, quality or quantity?

9. Does missing out on an activity or not being invited mean you are intentionally left out? What does jealousy do to your relationships?

10. What should be the main goal in relationships?

11. How can finding a higher purpose help you make friends? Why is this a better approach than trying to pursue someone specifically?

CHAPTER NINE

CYBERBULLIES

On January 18, 2019, a group of students from Covington Catholic High School in Kentucky attended the March for Life in Washington D.C. They came to speak up for the rights of the unborn, but their visit to Washington will instead be remembered for a controversy that exploded on social media.

On the last day of their trip to D.C., the students were involved in a conflict that was captured and distributed in fragments on social media. Initial videos surfaced of boys in a standoff with a single Native American man who was chanting while playing a drum. The man was a Vietnam war veteran and an Omaha tribe elder named Nathan Phillips. Some of the boys were chanting while one young man stood face to face with Mr. Phillips, a smile playing on his lips as he silently watched Mr. Phillips playing his drum.[80]

Initial reports interpreted the confrontation as a mob of angry young men threatening a defenseless, solitary Native American war veteran. Mr. Phillips himself appeared on several news outlets claiming that the students were taunting him and that he feared for his life. Social media was quick to judge. Comedian Kathy Griffin called for anyone who had information on these boys to "dox" them (i.e., release public information about them). Best-selling author Reza Aslan tweeted, "Honest question. Have you ever seen a more punchable face than this kids'?" He was speaking of the young man who had been facing Mr. Phillips. The media joined the critics and sided with Mr. Phillips' version of the story. Even the students' own school condemned their actions and apologized to Mr. Phillips.[81]

Then a longer video surfaced, giving the situation more context. In this more complete version of events, viewers can see that activists calling themselves Black Hebrew Israelites yelled profanities and racial epithets at the young students. That was when Mr. Phillips walked into the fray with his drum, accompanied by a cameraman. He walked right up to the young man who was smiling in the initial video and began playing his drum while staring into the student's face. Mr. Phillips was never in danger. He could have retreated in as many as three different directions. The new developments seemed to vindicate the young men and cast doubts on Mr. Phillips' version of the story.

Meanwhile, social media was busy assassinating the character of the Catholic students. Public enemy number one was the student who was standing face-to-face with Mr. Phillips. Someone misidentified him as Michael Hodge, and the bullies got to work. Michael's older brother, Andrew, responded on Twitter, giving us a perspective of what it's like to have social media turn on you.

> Yesterday was supposed to be a day of celebration for my middle brother Alex, who got married last night. Instead my family had to deal with the fallout of my youngest brother #MichaelHodge being falsely accused for standing & smiling in front of an indigenous man with a drum.... People then proceeded to spam my family with harassments and threats of physical violence. We then find out our parents (sic) address was posted online. If that wasn't enough, our family operated business has been slandered and attacked.... You reach out saying how "terrible" of a family we are, defame us, threaten us, and you know nothing about us. Yet you circulate the information and spam us like it is the only "truth" that has ever existed in your lives.... It saddens me people have nothing better to do on Saturday then (sic) scour the

internet for drama & then dig up info on a family & rile up an army to attack them. Hold yourselves to a higher standard, set a better example for your sphere of influence, we will all be better off for it.[82]

The real student was Nick Sandmann, a 16-year-old junior at Covington High. If the heat was intense for Michael Hodge, who wasn't even there, imagine what it was like for Nick. In a statement released following the media storm, he said,

I have received physical and death threats via social media, as well as hateful insults. One person threatened to harm me at school, and one person claims to live in my neighborhood. My parents are receiving death and professional threats because of the social media mob that has formed over this issue.[83]

On social media, haters are quick to judge. Once you are in their sights, your side of the story does not matter. It does not even matter if you are innocent. Mobs do not care about the truth. They are an unthinking mass of hatred.

Cyberbullies can take away your sense of safety, your reputation, and your self-esteem. Sometimes their assaults are even costlier. David Molak was a 16-year-old Eagle Scout who attended Alamo Heights High School in Texas. David had been receiving text messages from numerous bullies over a period of time. The bullies seemed to be motivated by nothing but meanness. Eventually, David, feeling there was no way out, took his own life. His older brother posted the following after David's death:

In today's age, bullies don't push you into lockers, they don't tell their victims to meet them behind the school's dumpster after class. They cower behind user names and fake profiles from miles away constantly berating and abusing good, innocent people.[84]

Another young student from Texas also committed suicide because of abuse. Brandy Vela started receiving ugly text messages from an untraceable smart phone application. Someone also made a fake Facebook page of her and set up an account on a dating website. The harassment focused mainly on Brandy's weight.[85]

We usually think of cyberbullying as targeting a young person in junior high or high school, but the targets can be the schools themselves with parents playing the role of the bully. Just last night, the principal at my son's school orientation had to plead with parents to come to teachers and administration when they had a problem instead of turning to social media. Schools, churches, retail stores, and other organizations are often unfairly maligned because of misunderstandings that could be resolved in just a few minutes of face-to-face conversation.

Countless other stories could be told. Bullying is on the rise. One study showed an increase of 52 percent in just four years (2003 to 2007). A 2014 study found that cyberbullying incidents tripled within a single year. Some research reports that one in five middle school students contemplate suicide as a solution to peer cruelty.[86] The Centers for Disease Control and Prevention indicated in 2017 that an estimated 14.9 percent of high school students are cyberbullied over the course of a year.[87] And teenagers do not hold a monopoly on this problem. A Pew Research Center study showed that 40 percent of adults have experienced some form of online harassment.[88] We long for the days when the trolls stayed under bridges, but now they are hiding in a seedier underground – in cyberspace, where their ambushes inflict more damage than the Billy Goats Gruff ever could have imagined.

What's Wrong with Bullying?

Bullies see victims as objects, not human beings.
The Bible teaches that we have all been created in the image of God (Genesis 1:26-28) and that we are special. Jesus tasted death for everyone (Hebrews 2:9). But bullies see people as a means to an end. Want to be the center of attention? Try to get laughs by making fun of an easy target. Feeling insecure? Pick on someone smaller than you. Bored? Entertain yourself by seeing how people react when they are hurt. Bullies use people for their own selfish purposes.

Bullying is hatred, not love.
Jesus gave His disciples a new commandment to love one another as He loved us. The world should know His disciples by their love (John 13:34-35). He even called us to love our enemies (Matthew 5:44). When bullies abuse and harass their victims, they are expressing hatred, not love. Many times they are simply passing on the hurt they received from others. They are like the fools described by Paul: "hated by others and hating one another." Christians are to turn away from all the hate and "speak evil of no one...avoid quarreling...be gentle...show perfect courtesy towards all people" (Titus 3:1-3).

Bullies use unkind words to exert power over others.
We tried to tell ourselves that sticks and stones are a bully's only weapons, but words really do hurt. Truth be told, words hurt worse than any physical punishment. The wise man said, "Death and life are in the power of the tongue..." (Proverbs 18:21), and James described the tongue as the strongest member of the body (James 3:1-6). The Bible says, "Let your speech always be gracious, seasoned with salt, so that you may know how you ought to answer each person" (Colossians 4:6). Our mouths are

for blessing others, not cursing them (Ephesians 4:29; James 3:10-12).

Bullying is an abuse of power.
To say that bullies abuse their power is not to say that they are particularly strong. A bully doesn't have to be above average. He just has to find somebody who seems smaller than him to pick on. Bullying is the Iron Rule: "might makes right." But how does God want the strong to treat the weak? He does not give people strength so they can crush those who are weaker than them. Strength is given to help others (Romans 15:1; Galatians 6:1-2).

Bullying is a violation of the Golden Rule.
Bullies live by the Iron Rule that says, "Might makes right," but Jesus taught, "So whatever you wish that others would do to you, do also to them, for this is the Law and the Prophets" (Matthew 7:12). Not even bullies want to be bullied. The Golden Rule and abuse cannot coexist.

How Can I Stop It?
Unfortunately, bullies will always hurt people online and off-line. One thing to remember is that it takes a victim to make a bully. When someone makes ugly comments about you, it is best to ignore them if you can. That doesn't mean the harassment and abuse won't sting. Even those with the toughest skin feel the scorn of mocking and rejection. Consider Jesus. He was like a sheep silent before its shearers (Isaiah 53:7). His captors grew more and more frustrated because He would not defend Himself during their unjust interrogations. Dumbfounded by Jesus' silence, Pilate cried, "Do you not hear how many things they testify against you?" But Jesus "gave him no answer, not even to a single charge, so that the governor was greatly amazed" (Matthew 27:13-14). The high priest was so frustrated by Jesus' lack of defense that he had one of his officers strike Jesus with

his hand (John 18:22). Because Jesus refused to be a victim, His bullies were embarrassed. Did Jesus' choice not to be a victim shield Him from the pain bullies inflict? No, He suffered, but He did not allow His suffering to empower His abusers (1 Peter 2:23).

Maybe you are the bystander instead of the victim. Is there anything that you can do? What are some things we can do to reduce the impact of bullying around us?

Learn how to identify it.
Michelle Borba teaches the definition of bullying using the acronym CAP:

- C – bullying is repeated *cruel* behavior.
- A – bullying is never *accidental*: the child who is bullying is intentionally causing another kid verbal, emotional, and/or physical pain.
- P – bullying is a *power* imbalance: the target cannot hold his own and needs help.[89]

Stay alert. Look for victims who need encouragement. Don't become an unwilling participant in a bully's scheme. Know what you are up against.

According to StopBullying.gov, cyberbullying produces new concerns. Unlike its real-world counterpart, cyberbullying is:

- *Persistent* – Digital devices offer an ability to immediately and continuously communicate 24 hours a day, so it can be difficult for children experiencing cyberbullying to find relief.
- *Permanent* – Most information communicated electronically is permanent and public, if not reported and removed. A negative online reputation, including for those who bully, can impact college admissions, employment, and other areas of life.

- *Hard to Notice* – Because teachers and parents may not overhear or see cyberbullying taking place, it is harder to recognize.[90]

Develop empathy for others.
Empathy is the ability to understand what others are feeling, even when you have not shared their experiences. Empathy is especially important in social media. The internet is not conducive to feeling for others. Online, we see digital versions of human beings stripped of the nonverbal cues that create empathy automatically in face-to-face conversation. We can become cruel without feeling the reaction our comment or post is causing.[91] Empathy makes you pause before firing off a nasty critique of someone's post or posting a hurtful joke at someone's expense. Developing an appreciation for what victims are feeling not only keeps you from becoming a bully but it can also embolden you to stand up for those who cannot fend for themselves.

Turn it around.
Social media is often viewed as a critical space, but it can be used to build others up. One teen got tired of seeing his peers bullied, so he created an anonymous account to tweet kind comments and let kids know someone out there cared. The results surpassed his expectations. Classmates began to copy his strategy, and they also posted kind tweets. Then a news station published the story. His "nice campaign" went viral. Teenagers from as far as Croatia, South Korea, and Australia started "nice" accounts to stop online bullying.[92] You don't have to stay caught up in the cycle of negativity online. Be a force for change. Say something nice. Others will follow your lead.

Cyberbullying is serious. People get hurt. Scars inflicted by bullies in youth are carried into adulthood. In extreme cases, people die. God did not put us on earth to hurt but to heal. Be careful what you post. Someone is on the other side, and they have feelings just like you do.

DISCUSSION

1. What are some cases of cyberbullying you have heard about?

2. What's wrong with bullying?

3. How do bullies use people as objects?

4. How is bullying a violation of Jesus' "new commandment"?

5. How do bullies use their mouths? How should a Christian speak to others?

6. How are we supposed to use our strength?

7. What is the Golden Rule, and how does it stop bullying?

8. How did Jesus respond to His bullies? Did His response shield Him from the hurt they inflicted?

9. Use the acronym CAP to define bullying.

10. What are some special concerns that go along with cyberbullying?

11. What is empathy? How can developing empathy help to stop bullies?

12. Does social media have to be all bad? What are some ways it can be used to encourage others?

PART FIVE

THE TREATMENT IS WORSE THAN THE DISEASE

CHAPTER TEN

MENTAL HEALTH

Self-centeredness is just one of the reasons why a person might spend hours on end, nose-down in her phone, scrolling, commenting, texting, and posting. Smartphone addiction could also be a desperate cry for help. Rates of teen depression and suicide have skyrocketed since 2011. Generation Z is on the brink of the worst mental health crisis in decades.[93] The irony is, while many teenagers are trying to cure their depression with social media, they may find that the treatment is worse than the disease.[94]

The science shows that one hour a day on social networks reduces satisfaction with overall life by 14 percent.[95] All screen activities are linked to less happiness, and all non-screen activities are linked to more happiness. Eighth-graders who spend ten or more hours a week on social media are 56 percent more likely to say they're unhappy than those who devote less time to social media. On the other hand, those who spend an above average time with their friends in person are 20 percent less likely to say they're unhappy than those who hang out with friends for a below average amount of time.[96]

The "social" part of social media is not the problem. Quite the opposite. Our brains are wired for connection. Our happiness may depend on relationships more than anything else. When compared with financial wealth, for example, social connections have a greater positive impact on our mental well-being.[97]

If it weren't for social media, some people would not have much social interaction at all. Over the last fifty years, there has been a steady decline in nearly every other social activity. People today are less likely to get married, volunteer, participate in social groups, go to church, or invite people into their homes.[98]

Bad Medicine

Can social media fill the relational void that is making us unhappy? The numbers don't lie. Social media is not getting the job done. But the problem isn't the social connections we are making. It seems to have something to do with the technology and what happens when you use it to engage with others.

At least five factors could potentially steal your joy when you log on.[99]

Envy

Paul warned that basing your self-esteem upon comparisons is unwise (2 Corinthians 10:12). Before the internet, such comparisons were limited, but now that we can scroll through hundreds of posts in a matter of minutes, the competition never ends. It's always Homecoming, we are the judge, and we always wind up giving ourselves the consolation prize.

Now more than ever, we must guard ourselves against envy, a sin that eats us from the inside out. Perhaps there is no more horrifying picture than the one we find in Ovid's tale of Minerva's visit to the house of Envy. Upon her arrival, Minerva catches Envy feeding on poisonous snakes. Here is how Ovid describes her:

> Stiffly she advances,
> and when she sees the beauty of the goddess
> and of her armor, she cannot help but groan,
> and makes a face, and sighs a wretched sigh.
> Then she grows pale, and her body shrivels up.
> Her glance is sidewise and her teeth are black;
> ...venom from her dinner coats her tongue;
> she only smiles at sight of another's grief,

nor does she know, disturbed by wakeful cares,
the benefits of slumber; when she beholds
another's joy, she falls into decay,
and rips down only to be ripped apart,
herself the punishment for being her.[100]

Envy is its own punishment. Measure yourself by someone else's carefully constructed online persona, and you will "fall into decay." You will be "ripped apart."

Our English word "envy" is derived from the idea of looking against, or eyeing with evil intent. After hearing the women sing, "Saul has struck down his thousands, and David his ten thousands," King Saul was very angry, and the Bible says "Saul kept an eye on David from that day on" (1 Samuel 18:9). That's envy. Paul included it among the works of the flesh (Galatians 5:19-21), but unlike the other vices he lists, envy tempts without promising pleasure. It eats at your soul until there's nothing left.

Confusion

Have you ever formed a strong opinion about something, only to find that it is quite easy to change your mind when you are confronted by someone holding a different point of view? Now imagine a whole crowd of people with competing viewpoints. That is what you have when you engage with others on social media. The opinions are endless, making it hard to form a strong opinion about anything.

The Roman philosopher Seneca anticipated the confusion we feel from social media long before the technology had been developed. In the first century, he wrote to his friend Lucilius,

You ask me to say what you should consider it particularly important to avoid. My answer is this: a mass crowd. It is something to which you cannot entrust yourself yet without risk.... I never come back home with quite the

111

same moral character I went out with; something or other becomes unsettled where I had achieved internal peace.[101]

The internet is great at disseminating information. Some of it is useful, some of it is interesting, some of it is false, and some of it is just plain terrible. If you log on before you have developed the art of critical thinking, you will be too easily inclined to confusion. It can be good for your preconceived notions to be challenged, as long as you have decided upon a standard for truth to serve as the foundation for your thinking. When Paul came to Berea, he brought new information. This could have set the people of Berea into a mental whirlwind. But they knew the Scriptures were true. Luke tells us, "Now these Jews were more noble than those in Thessalonica; they received the word with all eagerness, examining the Scriptures daily to see if these things were so" (Acts 17:11). They had a foundation for their thinking that gave them the ability to encounter new ideas without upsetting their whole worldview. If you lack that foundation, your mind will be in a constant state of disruption.

Guilt

I have already discussed the enormous amounts of time people are spending on social media every day. It could be that the time you spend networking online is crowding out other activities that could be more beneficial for your psychological well-being. Instead of getting together with friends, playing sports, serving at church, getting exercise, reading the Bible, or relaxing your mind, you might be stressing yourself out trying to keep up with your friends on Facebook or keeping your followers happy on Twitter and Instagram.

We know that staring at our smartphones is not the best use of our time, so after an hour or two (or more) of binging on social media, we unplug and feel guilty because we did not do something more valuable with our time. It's simple—meaningful activity feels good; worthless activity is depressing. Setting boundaries on screen time is crucial to keeping your mental health in good shape. If you stay in control, you will not feel that you have wasted your time.

Victimization

The longer individuals, particularly teens, spend on social media, the greater the chance of their becoming victims of cyberbullying. Every time you log onto your account, you open yourself up to attacks on your well-being and self-esteem. Because engaging online somehow depletes our empathy for other human beings, bullies are more prevalent in that space than in the real world. If you knew your worst enemy stood on the same street corner every day on your route to school, would you keep going the same way, or would you find a detour? Common sense says avoid the bully. Why not follow the same reasoning when we go online? The longer you hang out with the trolls, the more likely it is that they will turn on you.

Negativity

Social apps have developed a business model that combines technology and connectivity in order to provide their customers with information, pinpointed advertising, and even social reconstruction. Keep in mind that a social network's "customers" are different from its "users." The users are the millions of people logging onto the network and connecting with one another. The customers are the companies paying for access to our personal lives we voluntarily feed into the system.

When you log onto Facebook and scroll through your newsfeed, you are not looking at raw, untouched data organized according to the latest posts by your friends. That information has been fed through an algorithm that tailors it to benefit Facebook's customers.

Here is how it works. A large firm turns to Facebook for help in getting the attention of as many users as possible. What gets the most attention? Certainly not good news. The attention-grabbing headlines are almost always negative. So social apps like Facebook have developed algorithms designed to amplify negative emotions.[102] The system is designed to make you feel bad because that generates more money.

As these business models are being exposed, some social media titans are promising to change the way they do business so that they start improving society rather than harming it.[103] Time will tell whether their promises are sincere. Meanwhile, we cannot naïvely log onto a social network, thinking that we are engaging with a neutral system. This is capitalism, plain and simple. And you are the product.

Is There a Cure?

Where do we turn if our smartphones cannot make us happy? Are we doomed to misery? No, you can choose happiness. But is happiness a choice? God seems to believe so. We know this because of the various commands to rejoice that are found in the Bible. If joy were not a choice, the Lord would not have commanded it.

- "Rejoice greatly, O daughter of Zion! Shout aloud, O daughter of Jerusalem!" (Zechariah 9:9).
- "Make a joyful noise to the Lord, all the earth!" (Psalm 100:1).
- "Rejoice and be glad, for your reward is great in heaven" (Matthew 5:12).
- "Rejoice with those who rejoice" (Romans 12:15).
- "Rejoice in the Lord always; again I will say, Rejoice" (Philippians 4:4).
- "Rejoice always!" (1 Thessalonians 5:16).

- "Rejoice in so far as you share Christ's sufferings" (1 Peter 4:13).

Are these commands fair? Isn't joy an emotion? How can somebody control emotions? God would not ask us to do something outside of our capabilities. Perhaps if we gained a better understanding of the choice we are being asked to make, we would not feel we were being treated unfairly.

But before we get to the meaning of the joy God promises, we should ask, "Do I have the right to be unhappy?" Not long ago, I read a tweet in which someone crassly remarked that often people are unhappy because they are not living right. I am sure that much unhappiness does come from sin, but that is not the only source. Jesus grieved over death (John 11:33-35), hard hearts (Mark 3:5), others' sins (Luke 19:41-44), and suffering (John 12:27; Luke 22:39-46). The Son was merely following in the steps of His Father, who also grieves (cf. Genesis 6:6; Ephesians 4:30). There are times when it is natural for us to be unhappy. It just doesn't seem right, for example, to go to the funeral of a woman who has lost her husband of fifty years, put your hands on her shoulders, look her in the eyes, and say, "Cheer up! God wants you to be happy!"

In addition to natural grief, clinical depression can contribute to unhappiness through biological processes outside of our control. There are medications and treatments that can be helpful in this area, but we must show patience, love, and sympathy towards those who suffer from medical conditions that contribute to depression and anxiety. Furthermore, many unfortunate individuals have undergone trauma throughout their lives, through no fault of their own, and must cope with it for the rest of their lives. It takes more than a correction from a "miserable comforter" (cf. Job 16:2) to get them to "snap out of it." As Christians, we should never be so callous as to invalidate somebody's grief or, worse, call it a sin. After all, we are the ones

115

who have been commanded to "weep with those who weep" (Romans 12:15). How is that possible if God has made all unhappiness illegitimate?

Still, the Bible commands us to choose happiness. There must be some way to choose joy over sorrow.

Understanding the Promise

The commands listed above simply invite us to receive promises of happiness from God. In order to obey them, we need to understand exactly what God has promised. As we look at the terms used in Scripture, we will find that He is not offering cheap, momentary happiness based on circumstances. Neither does He guarantee that we will be shielded from pain and suffering. The following phrases will give us a clear picture of what God is asking us to choose.

"I shall not want" (Psalm 23:1)

Psalm 23 begins, "The Lord is my shepherd; I shall not want." *I shall not want* means total contentment, satisfaction, and abiding peace. In other words, David is saying, "I lack nothing." Contrast the peace of this psalm with the insatiable appetite of the world. Everywhere we look we see greed, lust, sexual immorality, and cruelty. The world craves and stops at nothing to get what it wants, but it never seems satisfied. Psalm 23 is about the promise we read in Philippians 4:19: "And my God will supply every need of yours according to his riches in glory in Christ Jesus." I may not get everything I desire, but with the Lord as my shepherd, every *need* will be fulfilled.

"Contentment" (1 Timothy 6:6-8; 2 Corinthians 12:9)

The New Testament word "contentment" indicates a self-sufficiency independent of any circumstance.[104] The contented believer gains strength from God, and that gives him satisfaction no matter what. Contentment does not come naturally. It has to be developed. Even Paul had to learn how to be content (Philippians 4:11).

"Blessed" (Matthew 5:3-12; Psalm 1:1-3; Revelation 14:13)
"Blessed," a term we know from Jesus' beatitudes, expresses a state of happiness, special favor, or privilege.[105] That may sound at first like high spirits, but look at the ways Jesus described blessedness in the beatitudes in Matthew 5:

- "The kingdom of heaven" (vv. 3, 10)
- "Comforted" (v. 4)
- "Inherit the earth" (v. 5)
- "Satisfied" (v. 6)
- "Receive mercy" (v. 7)
- "See God" (v. 8)
- "Called sons of God" (v. 9)

These are not simple emotions. Jesus is speaking of a deep, abiding blessedness that transcends our temporary experiences.

"Joy" (Philippians 1:3-5; 4:4; James 1:2-3; 1 Peter 4:12-13)
"Joy" sometimes refers to feelings and can result from circumstances, but for believers, joy is continuous because of our relationship with Christ.[106] We read Paul's commands to rejoice always and often feel that we come up short because we are not skipping down halls, singing happy songs, and greeting every person we meet with a permanent grin on our face. But examine carefully the words of Peter: "Though you do not now see him, you believe in him and rejoice with joy that is inexpressible and filled with glory" (1 Peter 1:8). Notice that Peter describes Christian joy in two ways: "inexpressible" and "filled with glory." A joy that is "inexpressible" cannot be indicated by a simple smile or a happy song. It cannot be expressed. It is internal, not external. External expressions of joy often depend upon

117

personality and culture. Peter is not worried about that. This joy is "filled with glory," which means it is given from heaven. It cannot be conjured up by even the most earnest disciples. Joy is a matter of grace.

The Source of Our Happiness

Joy in Christ is a satisfaction and peace in the love of God. Christ said,

> If you abide in me, and my words abide in you, ask whatever you wish, and it will be done for you. By this my Father is glorified, that you bear much fruit and so prove to be my disciples. As the Father has loved me, so have I loved you. Abide in my love. If you keep my commandments, you will abide in my love, just as I have kept my Father's commandments and abide in his love. These things I have spoken to you, that my joy may be in you, and that your joy may be full. (John 15:7-11)

In a similar passage, the apostle Paul writes,

> Through him we have also obtained access by faith into this grace in which we stand, and we rejoice in hope of the glory of God. Not only that, but we rejoice in our sufferings, knowing that suffering produces endurance, and endurance produces character, and character produces hope, and hope does not put us to shame, because God's love has been poured into our hearts through the Holy Spirit who has been given to us. (Romans 5:2-4)

As Christians, we are able even to rejoice in sufferings because the Holy Spirit has revealed God's Word to us in which we read about the love God showed us by sacrificing His Son on the cross.

His sacrifice means that not even death has a hold on us. Is that not cause for joy?

Do you believe that God loves you despite what you might have read on Facebook or Twitter? Can you believe that even when you are challenged by difficult circumstances and people in your life? Are you able to put your trust in Him even when you don't understand why your life has turned out the way that it has? Can you take comfort in the thought that even if things are out of your control, they are in the control of someone who is far wiser and more powerful than you? If so, you can rejoice always.

DISCUSSION

1. Does social media help with depression and anxiety? Explain your answer.

2. How is envy its own punishment?

3. Why do we feel guilty after binging on social media?

4. How is negativity built into a social network's business model?

5. Is happiness a choice? If not, why does God command it? If it is a choice, how are we able to control something that is commonly regarded as an emotion?

6. Are there ever any circumstances in which you have the right to be unhappy?

7. What kind of happiness does God promise?

8. What does Psalm 23:1 mean when it says, "I shall not want"?

9. What is "contentment" and how does it differ from what we usually regard as happiness?

10. Does the joy commanded by God have to be expressed in a certain way? What does the Bible mean when it commands us to rejoice?

CHAPTER ELEVEN

PHYSICAL HEALTH

"It's just dirt." That's what a friend of mine said about his hand after it had been amputated because of type 2 diabetes. Diabetes is so common, most people don't realize how serious it is. In some cases, it can cause the flesh to die in the extremities. That is what happened to my friend. He coped with the loss of his hand by focusing on the spirit. The body was disposable, he reasoned. He would soon be set free from his decaying mortal coil and go in his spirit to be with God. He was only half-right.

Our current bodies are in a state of irreversible decay. There is no stopping it. One day, unless the Lord intervenes first, our spirits will leave our bodies and, according to the beautiful description Jesus gave in the story of the rich man and Lazarus, be carried away to glory on angels' wings (Luke 16:22; cf. Ecclesiastes 12:7). Death is a separation of the body and spirit (James 2:26). But it is only a temporary separation. God has promised to redeem our bodies (Romans 8:23). When Jesus returns, every spirit that has ever been given life will rejoin its body in the resurrection (John 5:28-29; Acts 24:15). There is one caveat. The resurrected bodies of the righteous will be changed. No longer subject to disease and death, they will be glorified, transformed to be like Jesus' body so that they can live with God forever (1 Corinthians 15:42-57; Philippians 3:21; 1 John 3:2).

The Bible takes a higher view of the body than calling it "dirt." If the body were only dirt, God would not go to the trouble of bringing it back. We would continue to dwell like ghosts in misty realms. But God created us in the beginning as beings comprised of body and soul.

Because of the Bible's position on the body, we are supposed to pay attention to our physical health. Notice the emphasis upon the body in 1 Corinthians 6:19-20: "Or do you not know that your body is a temple of the Holy Spirit within you, whom you have from God? You are not your own, for you were bought with a price. So glorify God in your body." No one would desecrate a temple where he believes God dwells. Paul argues that our bodies are temples of the Holy Spirit, more precious than dirt, so we should glorify God in our bodies, never doing anything to harm them, but caring for them as best we can.

So far, I can't imagine anyone disagreeing with these points. Everyone likes a healthy body. Generally speaking, we feel better, live longer, and experience more when our bodies are healthy. But physical well-being comes at a price. You have to watch what you eat (I lost half of you right there). And you must also devote a lot of time and energy to healthy activities (there go the rest of you). It's no wonder America is suffering a growing health crisis, despite the wonders of modern medicine and the availability of healthcare.[107] We were busy already, but now we are spending nine hours a day online, and our digital habits are crowding out time needed for activities that promote good physical health, like exercise, hygiene, healthcare, and meal preparation.

To get a picture of the way social media has affected our bodies, we will look at four different areas of physical well-being: physical fitness, addiction, sleep deprivation, and safety.

Physical Fitness

Research shows that the more you use your phone, the less likely you are to be physically fit.[108] Childhood obesity has tripled in the United States since the 1970s. According to the Centers for Disease Control and Prevention, nearly one in five children (ages 6 to 19) is overweight.[109] It shouldn't take long for us to find an explanation for these numbers. We are putting smartphones into the hands of children as young as ten. The more you sit in front of the TV or stare into your phone, the less time you spend being physically active. Also, you spend less time eating square meals at the family table and more time munching on junk food and slugging high calorie soft drinks. The problem is time—our schedules have become unbalanced, giving too much time to online engagement and crowding out activities that promote wellness.

Many times, we turn to our phones because we think we haven't got anything better to do. Even if we decide that too much screen time is bad for us and make a sincere attempt to put our phones down, we return to them after a short respite, hungrier for a digital fix than we were before. Jesus told a parable in Matthew 12 about a demon that had been cast out of a person. It sought another place to rest, but found none, so it decided to return to its original host and happily found him vacant and open for business. Then what did the demon do? It went and found seven other spirits more evil than itself, and together they all possessed the man so that his condition became worse than before (vv. 43-45). Any attempt to kick a habit is doomed from the start if bad habits are not replaced by wholesome activities. Get interested in a hobby like sports, playing music, cooking, gardening, or volunteering at church. Develop new skills. Build something. Create. Collect. Read and write. Engage with others. Go outside and breathe the fresh air. There are things to do outside your phone. There are wonderful things to hold in your hands besides a game console.

Addiction

It is financially advantageous for the creators of social media platforms when people spend vast amounts of time online. It is only natural, then, for them to make their apps as fun and accessible as possible. In other words, *addictive.* Social media apps, like video games, are designed to hook their users and hold onto them as long as possible.[110]

Addiction may seem a better fit for a discussion of mental health, but science is discovering that habitual behavior has a significant connection to the neural processes occurring in the brain. Neural pathways are formed in the brain based on our behaviors. When we behave in a certain way repeatedly, these pathways grow stronger. With enough repetition, they become automatic. You can read a book or ride a bike, for example, without thinking about it because neural pathways have formed in your mind. This is what people mean when they speak of "muscle memory" to describe the practiced movements of an accomplished musician or a professional athlete.[111]

The good news is that we can create new neural pathways by changing our behavior. With repetition, pathways get stronger until the changes we are trying to make become the new normal. Maybe you have heard someone say that if you do something 21 days in a row, it becomes a habit. (The science says it is more like 66 days.[112]) This is a simplified explanation of how the brain physically changes with repeated behavior.

Many of us have become addicted to our devices without even knowing it. Ask the following three questions to see if your technology habits have begun to plow deep neural pathways in the grooves of your mind:

- Am I preoccupied with social media, the internet, video games, or technology?
- Am I unable to control my technology usage?
- Do I feel distress when I am unable to use my devices?[113]

If the answer to these questions is "yes," you have a problem. Addiction is serious. The apostle Peter explains that when a person is overcome by something, he has become a slave (2 Peter 2:19).

Odds are, if you spend too much time on social media, you already know it. So why is it so hard for us to change? The answer is in the neural pathways of the brain. Our brains are functioning on autopilot about 90 percent of the time. Changing habits requires a lot of effort to overcome the old ruts from years of behavior and create new, healthy pathways that steer us in the right direction.

Try these three suggestions to get control over your technology usage:

First, determine what practices should take the place of your excessive online habits. Write them down and set goals. Make a firm commitment to them so that you will take action.

Second, engage as much of the brain as possible as you try to change your neural wiring. Do this by soaking in new experiences using as many of the five senses as you can. Let's say you are trying to read the Bible more. Avoid negative thoughts while reading, and think about how honored you are to be reading God's Word. With positive emotions in place, engage the senses. Pay attention to the quietness of the moment. Feel the pleasure of a pen scratching notes in the margins. Enjoy the way the words look on the page. Breathe deeply as the peace of God settles in. Be mindful as you try to create new habits. This increases the chances of changing the circuitry in your brain.

Third, repeat. Neural pathways are created through the repetition of thoughts, feelings, and actions. At first, returning to wholesome behaviors will be agonizing. You're fighting habits that took a long time to develop. Also, you are exchanging instant gratification for practices that pay off long-term dividends. Be patient. Change takes time.

Sleep Deprivation

The Centers for Disease Control and Prevention recommends that school-age children get nine to twelve hours of sleep per day and that teens get eight to ten hours. It is recommended that adults sleep seven or more hours a day.[114] Technology has changed our sleep patterns. On the whole, Americans are getting far less sleep than they were a generation ago. The average teenager is sleeping fewer than six and a half hours per night. Over the course of the school year, students are deprived of so many hours of sleep that it adds up to about fifty missing nights of sleep per school year, making kids irritable, unable to focus, depressed, and anxious.[115]

Technology interferes with our sleep in three ways:[116]

- It displaces sleep time. Nearly every adolescent has at least one electronic device in his or her room, away from the watchful eyes of parents who might tell them to put away the device and get some sleep.[117]
- It causes increased emotional, cognitive, or physical stimulation, which disrupts sleep.
- The white-light illumination of phones, tablets, and other devices disrupts circadian rhythms (sleep cycles).

What's the big deal? What harm can losing a little sleep do? Quite a lot, as it turns out. Sleep deprivation leads to obesity, loss of focus, memory loss, and anxiety. Without sleep, you miss out on restorative processes that help the synapses of the brain and cognition. Also, growth hormones are secreted at a higher rate during sleep.[118] If you are losing sleep, it is affecting your health.

The best way to ensure that your technology is not interfering with your sleep is to set a bedtime and shut off devices one hour or more before that bedtime. Keep phones and tablets out of the bedroom overnight. Some parents like to set up a charging station in the kitchen or the living room, away from sleep areas. Stick to a routine as much as possible, sleeping and waking on a schedule.

Safety

Eighty-two percent of crimes committed by online predators originate from social networking sites.[119] As internet safety awareness has increased, predatory behavior has declined (53% between 2000 and 2010). Still, 9 percent of kids who use the internet have received an unwanted sexual solicitation.[120]

It is difficult to list the ways online predators try to connect with children and teens to lure them into face-to-face meetings. New apps are coming out every day. As of the writing of this book, the following apps are popular hideouts for dangerous creeps who want to harm young people.[121]

Yubo

Formally known as "Yellow," Yubo markets itself as "Tinder for teens" and encourages teens to form relationships by browsing through profiles from their area, swiping right for "yes" and left for "no." Users can chat or live stream videos of themselves in rooms that allow up to four friends and unlimited viewers. The minimum age for Yubo users is 13. The App Store warns of "infrequent/mild sexual content and nudity," which is enough to push conscientious users away from the app, but according to reports of those reviewing it, the inappropriate content is neither infrequent nor mild. Chats and video streams are never monitored, and users self-report their age by checking a box, which guarantees nothing and allows online predators to pose as children to form relationships under false pretenses.

IMVU

IMVU allows users to create avatars that can hang out with other players, chat, and interact with the virtual environments. IMVU users are allowed to chat with people they know, or by clicking "chat now," they are randomly connected to complete strangers. There are no filters built in to the program to block inappropriate content. Avatars often use profanity, dress in immodest clothing, and can even simulate explicit acts.

Kik Messenger

Kik is a messaging app based outside the U.S. that allows its users to interact with complete anonymity, since it requires no information to verify your identity. Kik has 300 million users and in 2017, 40 percent of teenagers in the U.S, were using it to send messages, pictures, videos, and other content.[122] Because Kik makes it easy to create fake accounts, browse accounts by age, and access to anyone's inbox, it's a popular app for pedophiles looking for victims.

Live.me

Live.me is a video streaming app allowing users to comment on one another's videos. Evil eyes lurk on the site, watching live streams and building trust with young users until they can coax them into streaming risky behavior, or even face-to-face meetings. Although there is an age restriction of 18 years or older, the age restrictions are easy to bypass. Live.me is full of explicit content. Worst of all, Live.me shares your location, making it easy for predators to hunt down their victims.

Omegle

Omegle is a chat room that is supposed to be for adults, 18 years and older, but as with the rest of the apps on this list, it is easy to get around the restrictions. The chat rooms are not monitored, so they are full of unwholesome conversations. Omegle's own website warns that "predators have been known to use Omegle, so please be safe."[123]

Snapchat

Originally intended by its developers to make sexting safe, Snapchat is the most popular app on this list, with more than 300 million monthly users.[124] Popular for its photo editing features, Snapchat was the first to introduce the disappearing post. "Snaps" vanish in fifteen seconds, giving users the illusion of secrecy, although a screenshot is all that is needed to capture any post, and even if your image is not captured, it's never actually deleted. A good hacker could retrieve it in no time. Thirty percent of Snapchat users say they use Snapchat because their parents don't.[125] Parents should be wary of allowing their kids to use an app with an agenda of secrecy and a mascot that is a ghost.

Social media apps are not the only hangouts for online bad guys. They will use any means at their disposal to try to connect with children and teens. Another common hunting ground is multiplayer videogames in which players connect through the internet. Whether it's social media, video games, chat rooms, or any other place on the internet, if it's a place where kids connect online, dangerous people will be lurking there.

Do not make the mistake of assuming that users on any online platforms are who they claim to be. It is easy to fake a profile. A friend of mine who worked with the Sheriff's Department used to give presentations about online safety. He would demonstrate how easy it was to set up a fake account by doing it within minutes in front of his audience. He would open up his computer, and a few clicks later he would be online as a 14-year-old girl. Before too long, strangers were trying to connect with him.

It is never safe to connect with strangers online. It is not normal for another user you do not know to ask for pictures, personal information, and especially face-to-face meetings. If someone tries to connect with you in this way, unfollow him immediately and report his behavior.

Parents, be nosy. A parent's first responsibility is to protect, not befriend. Snoop on your child's devices frequently and without warning. Let them know that you will be monitoring their use. Do not let them take tablets or phones to bed with them and teach them some basic guidelines of online safety. It is tough to protect your children, but if you don't, who will?

When used in moderation, social media can be a part of a healthy lifestyle. The key is balance. Prioritize your activities, making sure activities that are mentally, physically, and spiritually healthy are at the top of the list. If you do not have time for social media after you have completed the wholesome tasks that need to be done, you don't have time for social media. Period.

Remember, God is not done with you. You are going to need that body. So take care of it.

DISCUSSION

1. What is the Bible's position on the body?

2. How can social media lead to poor physical health?

3. Can you kick a bad habit without replacing it with wholesome activities? Explain.

4. How does repetitive behavior change the brain? What does this teach us about overcoming addictions?

5. What are some steps one can take to break bad habits and replace them with healthy ones?

6. Why is sleep important?

7. How do our devices interfere with sleep?

8. What can we do to ensure our technology does not interfere with healthy sleep cycles?

9. Go over the apps reviewed in this chapter. Are there others we should know about? What do dangerous apps have in common?

10. How can parents and children partner to promote healthy social media usage at home?

CHAPTER TWELVE

SPIRITUAL HEALTH

In 1934, the United States government formed the Federal Communications Commission (FCC) to regulate radio, television, wire, satellite, and cable communications. The commission was organized for a number of reasons, not least for public safety. The government decided that media made so many things possible, it had to be regulated and held accountable. Of course, the laws established by the FCC were democratic, not biblical, so they do not always align with Christian values, but the FCC's codes have at least served as a restraint on the sin and degradation made possible by broadcasting technology.

Things have changed. Unlike radio and television, the internet is not regulated by the United States government. While measures have been proposed, regulating the internet is trickier because of its global reach, concern for First Amendment rights, and its usefulness in giving minorities a voice. The good that has come from the internet cannot be calculated. Because of social media sites like Facebook and Twitter, oppressed populations have been able to broadcast their plights to the world, drawing much-needed attention that would have been impossible two decades ago. That is why many dictators place strict regulations upon internet communications. Tyrannical governments lose their control when the people have a voice.

As with anything, the freedoms made possible by the internet are a two-edged sword. Just as good messages travel at lightspeed throughout cyberspace, wicked ideas slither through binary pathways, looking for idle minds to deprave.

Families in Great Britain are concerned. A recent poll showed that more than half of parents believe social media harms their children's moral development. The study found that

- 60 percent had seen anger or hostility.
- 51 percent had seen arrogance.
- 41 percent saw bad judgment.
- 36 percent had seen hatred.

Most parents also reported a huge absence of humility, self-control, forgiveness, honesty, and fairness.[126]

At least parents can connect with their kids on social media and see what they are up to, right? Not exactly. Snapchat found a way to frustrate snoopy parents in 2011 by developing a social media platform in which "snaps" self-destruct ten seconds after they are opened, and "stories" vanish within 24 hours. Of course, Snapchat users should know that every picture posted to the internet is potentially permanent. Another user can take a screenshot of a suggestive or potentially embarrassing post, and everybody will be looking at it at school the next day. Why did developers create a social media platform with disappearing posts? There are a lot of great features in Snapchat (it has some of the best photo and video editing options in social media), but the basic premise of the software seems to be hiding pictures and content that could get you into trouble. Parents can monitor their child's social media activity on Facebook and Twitter by connecting with them and scrolling through their feeds. That is impossible on Snapchat.

We have already talked about the importance of keeping some secrets (see Chapter 7). Some things should stay private. But we hide other parts of our lives for less dignified reasons, to cover up shameful secrets. Jesus said,

For everyone who does wicked things hates the light and does not come to the light, lest his works should be exposed. But whoever does what is true comes to the light, so that it may be clearly seen that his works have been carried out in God. (John 3:20-21)

If you are hiding a picture from your parents, you probably should not be sharing it.

Because social media is such a big world, there are several areas of concern to discuss. We will not be able to address them all, but we will try to hit the most important challenges to Christian values.

Hatred and Cruelty

Early in 2018, YouTube star Logan Paul shared a video in which he laughed at the corpse of a suicide victim in Japan's Aokigahara forest. "Bro, did we just find a dead person in the suicide forest?" he says in the now-deleted video.[127] Paul has since apologized, but his behavior causes us to scratch our heads and ask, "How callous do you have to be to laugh at suicide?" Logan Paul's cruelty is disturbing enough, but perhaps even more concerning are his 18 million subscribers who watch him on a regular basis. Do they find this disdain for human dignity entertaining? Would they think suicide was funny if Logan Paul discovered the body of one of their loved ones?

Despite our sin and rebellion against him, God takes a very high view of humanity. From the beginning, He has strictly forbidden murder (Genesis 4:10; 9:6). David exclaims that he made us "a little lower than the heavenly beings" and crowned us with "glory and honor" (Psalm 8:5). Every person has been made in God's image (Genesis 1:27), so God shows no partiality (Acts 10:34-35). God loves His creation so much that He sent His only Son to die for the entire human race (John 3:16; Hebrews 2:9; 1 John 2:2).

God expects us to share His affinity for our fellow human beings. Hatred and cruelty are not to be tolerated. One of the greatest commands, second only to loving God with our hearts, souls, and minds is to "love your neighbor as yourself" (Matthew 22:39). We are even supposed to love our enemies (Matthew 5:44).

Social media users have proven to be innovative in finding fresh ways to be mean to others (see Chapter 9). A Christian should stand out by adhering to the Bible's instructions, such as:

- "Be kind to one another, tenderhearted, forgiving one another, as God in Christ forgave you" (Ephesians 4:32).
- "Put on then, as God's chosen ones, holy and beloved, compassionate hearts, kindness, humility, meekness, and patience, bearing with one another and, if one has a complaint against another, forgiving each other; as the Lord has forgiven you, so you also must forgive" (Colossians 3:12-13).
- "Let your speech always be gracious, seasoned with salt, so that you may know how you ought to answer each person" (Colossians 4:6).
- "Finally, all of you, have unity of mind, sympathy, brotherly love, a tender heart, and a humble mind" (1 Peter 3:8).

Sexual Immorality and Impurity

Every outlet is being used by the devil to tamper with impressionable minds. This includes social media. Most social media sites have standards they enforce, but the standards are established by worldly people with worldly concerns, not Christians trying to uphold God's Word. Don't be naïve. Social media is full of immodesty, sexual immorality, impurity, and sensuality.

It is impossible to live in this world without facing temptation. It is not a sin to unintentionally encounter temptation. It is sinful, however, to pursue sexual immorality. Jesus said, "But I say to you that everyone who looks at a woman with lustful intent has already committed adultery with her in his heart" (Matthew 5:28).

We are inundated with sexual immorality everywhere we turn. What are we to do? First of all, know that this is not a new problem. Social media may present new outlets for temptation, but purity has always been a challenge, and as long as the world stands, it will continue to be. Here are some suggestions from God's Word on how to keep your purity intact.

Make a covenant with your eyes.
In a list of ways he had been true to the Lord, Job said, "I have made a covenant with my eyes; how then could I gaze at a virgin?" (Job 31:1). Have you ever promised the Lord and yourself that you will do everything within your power to stay innocent of sexual sin? Some of us are afraid to make this promise because deep down we don't want to keep it. Any amount of indecision will guarantee failure. Purity starts with a commitment.

Do your best to avoid sinful influences.
The wise man said, "Do not enter the path of the wicked, and do not walk in the way of the evil. Avoid it; do not go on it; turn away from it and pass on" (Proverbs 4:14-15). Know where sin lurks and refuse to enter its quarters. If you follow a friend who is constantly posting immoral pictures and posts, unfollow him. The best way to defeat temptation is to avoid it.

Run!
Of course, it is not always possible to avoid temptation. That being the case, when confronted with sexual immorality, flee from it. That is the constant advice given throughout the Bible.

"Flee from sexual immorality" (1 Corinthians 6:18). "So flee youthful passions and pursue righteousness, faith, love, and peace, along with those who call on the Lord from a pure heart" (2 Timothy 2:22). This was Joseph's strategy when he was seduced by Potiphar's wife. He even ran out of his clothes to get away from her! His commitment to purity cost him dearly, but in the end it was worth the sacrifice. The Lord was always with Joseph because, among other things, Joseph had committed to honoring God with his body.

Repent when you fail.
Everyone sins. If and when you fall to temptation, start over by repenting and renewing your covenant with God. King David had a public and humiliating affair from which at first it did not seem he would recover. But thankfully David saw the importance of confession and repentance and renewed his commitment to God (Psalm 32:1-5; Psalm 51).

Profanity
Words are powerful. Solomon said that "life and death are in the power of the tongue" (Proverbs 18:21). Social media is a platform that gives everyone a voice, no matter who they are. All this power and accessibility make words and social media a potent combination. It is tempting to use strong language to get a reaction out of our audience.

Words are merely symbols, combinations of letters that when pronounced make distinct sounds. The organization of the sounds is called "language." The meaning of language is determined in the context of culture. That means the world around us determines the appropriateness of words and phrases. Christians should always be concerned about speaking appropriately. Proverbs 25:11 reads, "A word fitly spoken is like apples of gold in a setting of silver."

"Profanity" is language that is considered vulgar or inappropriate by society. It is tempting to use profanity on social media because the usual language doesn't always get the reaction we want. We get lazy and settle for any reaction at all. Wondering if there is anyone out there who notices us, we cuss and spew vulgarities. Suddenly, people are laughing. Or maybe they are mad or offended. It doesn't matter anymore because we are intoxicated by the attention. Someone might excuse bad language saying, "They're just words. They're not hurting anybody." But we have already established the power of words, and if society has determined that a word is inappropriate in certain contexts, it is wrong to use it in those places.

In Ephesians, Paul condemns certain kinds of talking. He says, "Let there be no filthiness nor foolish talk nor crude joking, which are out of place, but instead let there be thanksgiving" (5:4; cf. 4:25, 29). Paul encourages his readers to "walk as children of light" (v. 8). Most of us are pretty good at talking. Talking comes naturally, but Paul says, "Don't talk, walk as children of light." Does my language on social media reflect light or darkness? Asking that question will prevent inappropriate language from appearing on our newsfeeds.

Temptation abounds whether we are online or off-line. It is possible to defeat it. We just need to be prepared. Don't get caught off guard. Decide what kind of person you want to be before you post something to social media. Choose what you want to take into your heart before you look. A few simple choices can make a big difference.

DISCUSSION

1. Can you rely upon the law to make the internet spiritually safe?

2. What are some of the biggest moral concerns on social media as you see it?

3. What are some good reasons for keeping things secret? What are some of the kinds of secrets we should not be keeping?

4. What is God's view of humanity? How should we view our fellow human beings? Is there something to value in every soul?

5. How can you use social media to show kindness and love towards others?

6. What are some examples of the kind of impurity you might encounter on social media?

7. Give some suggestions on how to keep your purity intact online.

8. Can you expect to be perfect? What should you do when you fail?

9. What is profanity? Why is it wrong?

10. What measures can you take to ensure that your language is respectful and appropriate?

PART SIX

BUILDING A SOCIAL MEDIA CONTRACT

CHAPTER THIRTEEN

MAKE A PACT

We have covered a lot of ground, from issues caused by our infinite appetite for distractions to identity crises. We have discussed friends and bullies and have addressed mental, physical, and spiritual health. How do we convert what we have learned into a plan that will incorporate social media into a balanced, healthy lifestyle in which God receives the honor He deserves?

Do we get rid of our phones? No, our phones are not the problem. The issues that surface from social media are rooted deeply in the soil of our hearts, as I hope this book has shown.

Do we throw up our hands and abandon all hope of conquering the problems we are having with our technology? Do we make excuses like, "It's the world we live in. What can we do about it?" Neither of these extremes is realistic or responsible. There is a better solution. *We write a social media contract.*

Writing a social media contract forces you to think about social media as a tool instead of passively allowing it to become your master. As you are making it, you should be asking, "What am I hoping to gain from social networking?" Maybe you want to keep up with your family and see those cute pictures of your nieces, nephews, or grandchildren. Do you want to stay up-to-date on the news? Communicate with friends? Are you interested in social media platforms as networks for your business? Do you want to advertise? Are there spiritual benefits to networking online? Maybe it's the way you stay connected to your church and listen to lessons from classes and worship services. Can you use apps like Facebook, Instagram, and Twitter to learn about culture, art, and music? Are these tools good ways to stay informed about your schools, clubs, and organizations? Do you just want to socialize? Is it your favorite form of entertainment? What do you want? A social media contract will put you in the captain's chair of your online experience instead of turning you into a slave. If you don't assume control, the internet will become your master, and it wields a whip with a vicious sting.

Your contract has to stay simple. If it's too complicated, you are doomed to fail from the start. Come up with a few goals you can internalize and stick to them.

In the beginning, you will have to look at your contract often. You may want to put it in a prominent place. Remember the Bible's teaching on renewal (Romans 12:2; 2 Corinthians 4:16; Ephesians 4:23; Colossians 3:10). Concepts don't sink in the first time you hear them. You must remind yourself about them daily. At first, changing your thinking and behavior is very difficult, but with time, behavior you thought you could never adopt becomes second nature.

This will be a contract with yourself, but your chances for success improve exponentially if you find someone who will keep you accountable. Most successful people can count four or five mentors who have been influential in their lives.[128] Find a friend who is willing to check in with you from time to time and who will listen to your successes and failures. If the first person you pick does not work out, don't give up on finding a partner. Ask somebody else to help.

What sort of guidelines should you include in your social media contract? It may be helpful to think in terms of a PACT: Priorities, Areas, Conduct, and Time.

Priorities

What's important to you? What are the things in your life that you cannot do without? Hopefully, God is at the top of the list. Everything in life must come after Him because He is the only one who is capable of occupying first place in your heart. An idol

144

is anything you put before the Lord. We must be careful about idols because we tend to resemble our objects of worship.

> The idols of the nations are silver and gold, the work of human hands. They have mouths, but do not speak; they have eyes, but do not see; they have ears, but do not hear, nor is there any breath in their mouths. Those who make them become like them, so do all who trust in them. (Psalm 135:15-18)

Is social media something you would like to resemble? It has its good points, but it is also a hotbed of hatred, self-obsession, wasted time, worldliness, and frivolity.

Only God is qualified to be first place in your heart. He is powerful, wise, faithful, loving, and full of mercy. Who would not want to become like that?

Once you reorder your priorities so that God is first, decide what follows. What are your goals in life? What do you want to spend your time doing? Has social media become a distraction keeping you from accomplishing these goals? Decide what should come first in life and include that in your social media contract.

Areas

Where will you use social media? Most of us do not ask ourselves this question, but it is very important. There are obvious places where social media should be off-limits: during church and Bible classes, in school while you are supposed to be studying, and in front of a friend or family member who is trying to converse with you.

Family dinners used to be semi-formal occasions. Everyone ate at the same time, the kids were told to mind their manners, and you could not leave before asking, "May I be excused?" Today, families rarely gather around the table to eat together, and when they do, they usually bring their devices with them. This may seem harmless, but mealtime is one of the few occasions for families to commune together. Research has shown that family meals are an indicator of a child's long-term success.[129] Smartphones interrupt these valuable moments in significant ways. Because of the frequent distraction caused by the bleeps of notifications and our compulsion to respond immediately to texts and tweets, dinner conversations tend to be superficial when devices are present. Meals last only a few minutes. Don't take your phone to the table. It can wait until after dessert.

Never fiddle with your phone while driving! Distracted driving accounts for 25 percent of all motor vehicle fatalities and 58 percent of teen crashes. According to the Department of Motor Vehicles, nine people a day die in car accidents involving distracted driving. It takes only three seconds for a car crash to occur after a driver's attention has been diverted.[130] Yet most drivers admit to texting, checking email, surfing the net, and other dangerous behaviors while they are behind the wheel. Why? Distracted driving may be the most preventable cause of death in the world. If we all decided not to use our phones while driving before we get into our cars, there would be far fewer fatalities on the road.

We have already noted that Americans are suffering from a sleep deprivation epidemic. Teens are supposed to be getting eight to ten hours of sleep per night, but the average teenager in the U.S. is getting about six and a half hours of sleep. It is best not to take phones and tablets into your bedroom. Screen use is safer in public places. Isolation breeds temptation.[131] But if you do use devices in sleep areas, kick them out before bedtime. Some families find it helpful to set up a charging station in a central location of the house where everyone's devices can stay plugged in overnight. This reduces the temptation of carrying your phone to bed with you. The goal is to prevent messages and notifications from disturbing your sleep or having a digital toy nearby, tempting you from getting the sleep that you need.

Conduct

We should discipline ourselves to behave in a godly way no matter where we are, but this seems to be especially important online. For some reason, we tend to engage in riskier behavior when we are in front of a computer screen. Perhaps it's the illusion of anonymity, or maybe we forget there is another person on the other side of the screen.

Behavior improves when we think ahead. As you write your social media contract, ask yourself how you would like to behave when interacting with others online. What kind of language should you use? Will your words be "seasoned with salt"? (Colossians 4:6). Practice the Golden Rule (Matthew 7:12). How would you like others to treat you? Decide that you will treat them the same way. How much will you share with others? What parts of your life should you keep private? Would you be embarrassed for a potential college admissions rep, employer, or spouse to see what is in your feed?

Time

"Make the best use of the time," Paul says, "because the days are evil" (Ephesians 5:16). Time is like a wild horse – it will run away from you if you do not bridle it. When I first began to research the impact social media was making upon society and Christian faith, I expected the biggest threats to be in the categories of identity, immorality, empathy, and relationships. And these are all very serious challenges discussed in this book. What I did not expect to find was the effect social media was having on our time. In the amount of time the average person spends on social media during his life, a person could make 32 trips to the moon and back! Are we making the best use of our time?

What is the maximum amount of time you will allow yourself to spend on social media? It may be more useful to set goals for how much time you will spend on your priorities. For example, how much time would you like to spend reading the Bible, praying, exercising, or doing your homework? Schedule the most important things first, and then you can check in with your friends on social media.

Set a bedtime and try as hard as you can to live by it. Keep in mind that the average adult needs seven or more hours of sleep per day. Also, you should set a time to unplug 30 minutes to an hour before your bedtime. This gives your mind and body a chance to wind down for sleep.

Look at the example of a social media contract on the next page. You do not have to use this form; something else may work better for you. The important thing is to make a contract with yourself that is simple, realistic, and effective.

MY SOCIAL MEDIA CONTRACT

I, _____, will make a PACT with myself to…

Set Priorities
The most important priority to me is
_____.

Other priorities I want to remember are:
_____
_____
_____

Designate Areas
I will not use social media in…
_____
_____
_____

I will designate a place to leave my phone outside my bedroom overnight.

Watch My Conduct

My words will be _____

My eyes will look _____

My intentions will be _____

My friends / followers will be _____

My posts will be _____

My pictures will be _____

Set Time Limits

List some activities that fit your priorities and how much time you plan to spend on each one.

Activity   Time

_____   _____

_____   _____

_____   _____

I will go to bed at _____.

I will "unplug" by _____.
(suggestion: 30 min. to 1 hr. before bedtime)

I will honor this contract to the best of my ability.

Signed,

_____

DISCUSSION

1. How can a social media contract help you?

2. What are some good uses of social media?

3. Why is it helpful to enlist the support of someone who will help keep you accountable?

4. What does the acronym PACT stand for?

5. What sort of priorities should we be making? Why should we be careful about what comes first?

6. What places should be off limits for digital devices? Where are some good spots to log on?

7. How should Christians conduct themselves online?

8. How much time are you spending on social media? Do you think you are above or below the average?

9. Do you think phones and tablets contribute to sleep deprivation? Is it necessary to leave them out of the bedroom overnight?

10. What are some things you can do to stick to your social media contract?

ENDNOTES

Preface

[1] Alex Suskind, "15 Years After Napster: How the Music Service Changed the Industry," *Daily Beast* (June 6, 2014), www.thedailybeast.com/15-years-after-napster-how-the-music-service-changed-the-industry (accessed November 17, 2018).

[2] Jeremy Wade Morris, *Selling Digital Music, Formatting Culture* (University of California Press, 2015), 116.

[3] Mark Harris, "The History of Napster," *Lifewire* (August 13, 2018), www.lifewire.com/history-of-napster-2438592 (accessed November 17, 2018).

[4] Ken Sundheim, "Where They Started, the Beginning of Facebook and Twitter: A Brief History of Social Media," *Business Insider* (August 5, 2011), www.businessinsider.com/a-brief-history-of-social-media-2011-7 (accessed November 14, 2018).

[5] Kabir Sehgal, "Spotify and Apple should become record labels so musicians can make a fair living," *CNBC* (January 26, 2018), www.cnbc.com/2018/01/26/how-spotify-apple-music-can-pay-musicians-more-commentary.html (accessed November 14, 2018).

[6] Sundheim.

[7] Jean Twenge, "Have Smartphones Destroyed a Generation?" *The Atlantic*, https://www.theatlantic.com/magazine/archive/2017/09/has-the-smartphone-destroyed-a-generation/534198/ (accessed November 9, 2017), and Tony Reinke, "Twelve Tips for Parenting in the Digital Age," *Desiring God*, www.desiringgod.org/twelve-tips-for-parenting-in-the-digital-age (accessed June 20, 2018).

Chapter 1: Social Studies

[8] J.R.R. Tolkien, *The Lord of the Rings* (Houghton Mifflin Co., 1994), 72.

[9] Tom Standage, *Writing on the Wall: Social Media—The First 2,000 Years* (2013), 3-4.

[10] Jean Twenge, "Have Smartphones Destroyed a Generation?" *The Atlantic*, https://www.theatlantic.com/magazine/archive/2017/09/has-

the-smartphone-destroyed-a-generation/534198/ (accessed November 9, 2017).

[11] John Stonestreet and Brad Knuckle, *A Practical Guide to Culture: Helping the Next Generation Navigate Today's World* (2017), loc 1431.

[12] Angela Moon, "Two-thirds of American adults get news from social media: survey," *Reuters* (September 8, 2017), www.reuters.com/article/us-usa-internet-socialmedia/two-thirds-of-american-adults-get-news-from-social-media-survey-idUSKCN1BJ2A8 (accessed November 13, 2018).

[13] Kevin Granville, "Facebook and Cambridge Analytica: What You Need to Know as Fallout Widens," *The New York Times* (March 19, 2018), www.nytimes.com/2018/03/19/technology/facebook-cambridge-analytica-explained.html (accessed November 27, 2018).

[14] Sheera Frenkel, Nicholas Confessore, Cecilia Kang, Matthew Rosenberg and Jack Nicas, "Delay, Deny and Deflect: How Facebook's Leaders Fought Through Crisis," *The New York Times* (November 14, 2018), www.nytimes.com/2018/11/14/technology/facebook-data-russia-election-racism.html (accessed November 27, 2018).

[15] Some studies show that the cognitive impact of digital technology is not totally negative. Social media, used in moderation, can promote a greater knowledge base, improved language and literacy, and improved ability to organize information (Jodi Gold, *Screen-Smart Parenting: How to Find Balance and Benefit in Your Child's Use of Social Media, Apps, and Digital Devices* (2015), 44.

[16] Clive Thompson, *Smarter Than You Think: How Technology Is Changing Our Minds for the Better* (2013), 231.

[17] Jaron Lanier, *Ten Arguments for Deleting Your Social Media Accounts Right Now* (2018), 36.

[18] Matthew Ellis, "Social Media in the 2016 U.S. Presidential Election," *E-International Relations Students* (July 28, 2017), https://www.e-ir.info/2017/07/28/social-media-in-the-2016-u-s-presidential-election/ (accessed November 27, 2018).

[19] Ibid.

[20] See Tom Standage, *Writing on the Wall* (2013), 233-4, and Robin Smith, "These Countries Censor Websites Like Facebook And YouTube," *Daily Infographic* (April 11, 2018), www.dailyinfographic.com/2018-internet-censorship (accessed November 27, 2018).

[21] Andrew Conrad, "10 Powerful Church Statistics on Social Media Use," *Capterra* (March 13, 2018), https://blog.capterra.com/church-statistics-social-media/ (accessed November 27, 2018).

[22] Tony Reinke, *12 Ways Your Phone Is Changing You* (Crossway, 2018), 72.

[23] Sherry Turkle, *Alone Together* (Basic Books, 2011).

[24] Twenge.

Chapter 2: Focus

[25] Aldous Huxley, "Brave New World Revisited" (1958), https://www.huxley.net/bnw-revisited/ (accessed January 29, 2019).

[26] Tony Reinke, *12 Ways Your Phone Is Changing You* (Crossway, 2018), 41.

[27] Sherry Turkle, *Alone Together* (Basic Books, 2011), 161.

[28] "Distracted Driving," *National Highway Traffic Safety Administration*, www.nhtsa.gov/risky-driving/distracted-driving (accessed August 31, 2018).

[29] Quoted in Tony Reinke, "Turn My Eyes from Worthless Things: Curbing Our Infinite Appetite for Distraction," *Desiring God* (May 29, 2017), www.desiringgod.org/articles/turn-my-eyes-from-worthless-things (accessed July 11, 2018).

[30] Turkle, 202.

[31] Edmund Morris, *The Rise of Theodore Roosevelt* (Random House, 1979), 263-4.

[32] Quoted in William Powers, *Hamlet's Blackberry: Building a Good Life in the Digital Age* (Harper Perennial, 2010), 42.

[33] Robert Alter, *The Book of Psalms* (W.W. Norton & Co., 2007), 165.

[34] Powers, 58-9.

[35] Reinke, "Turn My Eyes."

[36] Ralph Earle, *Word Meanings of the New Testament* (Beacon Hill, 1987), 66.

Chapter 3: Time

[37] Fyodor Dostoevsky, *Crime and Punishment* (trans. Constance Garrett; 1848), 178.

[38] Hayley Tsukayama, "Teens spend nearly nine hours every day consuming media," *The Washington* Post (November 3, 2015), www.washingtonpost.com/news/the-switch/wp/2015/11/03/teens-spend-nearly-nine-hours-every-day-consuming-media/?noredirect=on&utm_term=.71f624cb8743 (accessed July 6, 2018).

[39] Evan Asano, "How Much Time Do People Spend on Social Media?" *Social Media Today* (January 4, 2017), www.socialmediatoday.com/marketing/how-much-time-do-people-spend-social-media-infographic (accessed July 6, 2018).

[40] John Maxwell, *Today Matters* (Warner Faith, 2004), 67.

[41] Ralph Earle, *Word Meanings in the New Testament* (Beacon Hill, 1987), 322.

[42] Jerry Sittser, *The Will of God as a Way of Life* (Zondervan, 2004), 150.

[43] Philip Larkin, "Days," *Poetry Foundation*, https://www.poetryfoundation.org/poems/48410/days-56d229a0c0c33 (accessed July 6, 2018).

[44] *Meditations* 2:14.

[45] C.S. Lewis, *The Screwtape Letters* (Macmillan Publishing Co., 1982), 56.

[46] Norman MacLean, *A River Runs through It and Other Stories* (2017), 4.

[47] Mark Galli, "I Wasted My Time With This. So Should You," *Christianity Today* (July/August 2017), 75-8.

Chapter 4: Boundaries

[48] Marvin Vincent, *Vincent's Word Studies in the New Testament*, 3:237.

⁴⁹ M.T, Anderson, *Feed* (Candlewick Press, 2002), 37.

⁵⁰ Timothy Keller, *The Reason for God* (Dutton, 2008), 47.

⁵¹ Jean M. Twenge and W. Keith Campbell, "Associations between screen time and lower psychological well-being among children and adolescents: Evidence from a population-based study," *Preventive Medicine Reports* (December 2018), www.sciencedirect.com/science/article/pii/S2211335518301827 (accessed December 18, 2018).

⁵² Jonathan McKee, *The Teen's Guide to Social Media* (Shiloh Run Press, 2017), 111.

⁵³ Jean Twenge, "New findings add twist to screen time limit debate," *The Conversation* (November 6, 2018), https://theconversation.com/new-findings-add-twist-to-screen-time-limit-debate-105717 (accessed November 13, 2018).

⁵⁴ McKee, 132-33.

⁵⁵ Francis Schaeffer, *The Complete Works of Francis A. Schaeffer: A Christian Worldview, Volume One, A Christian View of Philosophy and Culture* (Crossway, 1982), 369.

Chapter 5: Who Are You?

⁵⁶ Sherry Turkle, *Alone Together* (Basic Books, 2011), 273.

⁵⁷ Robert S. McGee, *The Search for Significance* (Rapha Publishing, 1990), 196.

Chapter 6: Selfies

⁵⁸ "Selfie Obsession: The Rise of Social Media Narcissism [INFOGRAPHIC]," *Rawhide* (December 29, 2015), www.rawhide.org/blog/infographics/selfie-obsession-the-rise-of-social-media-narcissism/ (accessed August 24, 2018).

⁵⁹ Dietrich Bonhoeffer, *The Cost of Discipleship* (SCM Press, 1959), loc. 3940.

⁶⁰ "Ellen DeGeneres hits back against 'gay agenda' accusations," *CBS News* (January 14, 2015), www.cbsnews.com/news/ellen-degeneres-

hits-back-against-gay-agenda-accusations/ (accessed November 14, 2018).

[61] William Shakespeare, "Hamlet" (1:3).

[62] Flannery O'Connor, "My Dear God: A Young Writer's Prayers," *The New Yorker* (September 16, 2013), https://www.newyorker.com/magazine/2013/09/16/my-dear-god (accessed February 5, 2019).

[63] I heard the "bully or a baby" illustration in a lecture given by Dale Jenkins at the Freed-Hardeman lectures in 2014.

Chapter 7: Profiles

[64] Scott Jaschik, "Social Media as 'Fair Game' in Admissions," *Inside Higher ED* (April 23, 2018), www.insidehighered.com/admissions/article/2018/04/23/new-data-how-college-admissions-officers-view-social-media-applicants (accessed July 23, 2018).

[65]Clive Thompson, *Smarter Than You Think: How Technology Is Changing Our Minds for the Better* (Penguin Press, 2013), 210.

[66] Wendy Shalit, *A Return to Modesty* (Touchstone, 1999), 135.

[67] Ibid., 136.

[68] Chris Ridgway, "Fixing Our Privacy Settings," *Christianity Today* (September 2018), 29-35.

[69] N.T. Wright, *Paul: A Biography* (HarperOne, 2018), 18.

Chapter 8: Friends

[70] E.M. Forster, *The Machine Stops* (Golden Deer Classics, 1909), 3.

[71] Jean Twenge, "Have Smartphones Destroyed a Generation?" *The Atlantic*, https://www.theatlantic.com/magazine/archive/2017/09/has-the-smartphone-destroyed-a-generation/534198/ (accessed November 9, 2017).

[72] Quoted in Tony Reinke, "Twelve Tips for Parenting in the Digital Age," *Desiring God*, www.desiringgod.org/twelve-tips-for-parenting-in-the-digital-age (accessed June 20, 2018).

[73] Isaac Asimov, *The Naked Sun* (Bantam Books, 1957), 128-9.

[74] Greg Ogden, *Transforming Discipleship* (Inter-Varsity Press, 2003), 127.

[75] "Marriage and Divorce," *The American Psychological Association*, www.apa.org/topics/divorce/ (accessed August 17, 2018).

[76] Alan Loy McGinnis, *The Friendship Factor* (Augsburg, 1979), 15.

[77] Henry David Thoreau, *The Journal of Henry David Thoreau, 1837-1861* (New York Review Books Classics, 2009), 451.

[78] Andrew Sullivan, *Love Undetectable: Notes on Friendship, Sex, and Survival* (Knopf, 1998), 195.

[79] C.S. Lewis, *The Four Loves* (HarperOne, 2017).

Chapter 9: Cyberbullies

[80] "After Covington Catholic students caught in social media maelstrom, fuller picture emerges," *Catholic News Agency* (January 21, 2019), www.catholicnewsagency.com/news/after-covington-catholic-students-caught-in-social-media-maelstrom-fuller-picture-emerges-30604 (accessed January 23, 2019).

[81] Douglas Ernst, "Ben Shapiro rips 'manufactured media lie' against Covington Catholic High School boys," *The Washington Times* (January 21, 2019), www.washingtontimes.com/news/2019/jan/21/ben-shapiro-rips-manufactured-media-lie-against-co/ (accessed January 23, 2019).

[82] Chris Menahan, "Family of Teen Falsely IDed as Covington Student Tells of Harrassment by Twitter Mob," *Infowars* (January 21, 2019), www.infowars.com/family-of-teen-falsely-ided-as-covington-student-tells-of-harrassment-by-twitter-mob/ (accessed January 23, 2019).

[83] "Statement of Nick Sandmann, Covington Catholic High School junior, regarding incident at the Lincoln Memorial," *CNN* (January 23, 2019), www.cnn.com/2019/01/20/us/covington-kentucky-student-statement/index.html (accessed January 23, 2019).

[84] "Real Life Stories," *Pure Sight Online Child Safety*, www.puresight.com/Real-Life-Stories/david-molak-2000-2016-puresight.html (accessed August 14, 2018).

[85] "Cyberbullying pushed Texas teen to commit suicide, family says," *CBS News* (December 2, 2016),

www.cbsnews.com/news/cyberbullying-pushed-texas-teen-commit-suicide-family/ (accessed August 10, 2018).

[86] Michelle Borba, *Unselfie: Why Empathetic Kids Succeed in Our All-About-Me World* (Touchstone, 2016), xv.

[87] "What Is Cyberbullying?" *StopBullying.gov*, www.stopbullying.gov/cyberbullying/what-is-it/index.html (accessed August 10, 2018).

[88] Jerry Carino, "Cyberbullied at 53, she's looking to start a Jersey Shore support group for adults," *APP.* (April 20, 2018), www.app.com/story/news/local/how-we-live/2018/04/20/adult-cyberbullying-support-group/523284002/ (accessed August 14, 2018).

[89] Borba, 173.

[90] "What Is Cyberbullying?" *StopBullying.gov*, www.stopbullying.gov/cyberbullying/what-is-it/index.html (accessed August 10, 2018).

[91] Jaclyn Parrish, "How to Not Be an Online Troll," *The Gospel Coalition* (May 14, 2018), www.thegospelcoalition.org/article/not-online-troll/ (accessed May 14, 2018).

[92] Borba, 211.

Chapter 10: Mental Health

[93] Jean M. Twenge, "Have Smartphones Destroyed a Generation?" *The Atlantic* (September 2017), www.theatlantic.com/magazine/archive/2017/09/has-the-smartphone-destroyed-a-generation/534198/ (accessed August 3, 2018).

[94] Christina Sagioglou and Tobias Greitemeyer, "Facebook's emotional consequences: Why Facebook causes a decrease in mood and why people still use it," *Computers in Human Behavior* (June 2014), www.sciencedirect.com/science/article/pii/S0747563214001241 (accessed December 11, 2018).

[95] Emily McDool, Philip Powell, Jennifer Roberts, and Karl Taylor, "Social Media Use and Children's Well-being," *Institute of Labor Economics* (December 2016), https://papers.ssrn.com/sol3/papers.cfm?abstract_id=2886783 (accessed December 11, 2018).

[96] Twenge.

[97] Matthew Lieberman, *Social: Why Our Brains Are Wired to Connect* (Broadway Books, 2013), 241-7.

[98] Ibid., 248.

[99] The first three of these are theorized in McDool, Powell, Roberts, and Taylor.

[100] Ovid, Charles Martin, trans., *Metamorphoses* (II:1065-1078).

[101] William Powers, *Hamlet's Blackberry: Building a Good Life in the Digital Age* (Harper Perennial, 2010). 110.

[102] Jaron Lanier, *Ten Arguments for Deleting Your Social Media Accounts Right Now* (Henry Holt & Co., 2018), 26-7.

[103] Josh Constine, "Facebook will change algorithm to demote 'borderline content' that almost violates policies," *Tech Crunch* (November 15, 2018), https://techcrunch.com/2018/11/15/facebook-borderline-content/ (accessed December 11, 2018).

[104] Ralph Earle, *Word Meanings in the New Testament* (Beacon Hill, 1987), 347.

[105] William D. Mounce, *Mounce's Complete Expository Dictionary of Old & New Testament Words* (Zondervan, 2006), 70.

[106] Ibid., 369.

Chapter 11: Physical Health

[107] National Research Council (US); Institute of Medicine (US); Woolf SH, Aron L, eds., U.S. Health in International Perspective: Shorter Lives, Poorer Health (2013), www.ncbi.nlm.nih.gov/books/NBK154469/ (accessed January 19, 2019); and Julie Beck, "Less Than 3 Percent of Americans Live a 'Healthy Lifestyle'," The Atlantic (March 23, 2016), www.theatlantic.com/health/archive/2016/03/less-than-3-percent-of-americans-live-a-healthy-lifestyle/475065/ (accessed January 19, 2019).

[108] Ana Homayoun, *Social Media Wellness: Helping Tweens and Teens Thrive in an Unbalanced Digital World* (2018), 169.

[109] *Centers for Disease Control and Prevention*, "Childhood Obesity Facts," www.cdc.gov/healthyschools/obesity/facts.htm (accessed January 16, 2019).

[110] Homayoun, 162.

[111] Julie Hani, "The Neuroscience of Behavior Change," *Health Transformer* (August 8, 2017), https://healthtransformer.co/the-neuroscience-of-behavior-change-bcb567fa83c1 (accessed January 18, 2019).

[112] "How Long Does it Take for Something to Become a Habit?" *Examined Existence*, https://examinedexistence.com/how-long-does-it-take-for-something-to-become-a-habit/ (accessed January 18, 2019).

[113] Jodi Gold, *Screen-Smart Parenting: How to Find Balance and Benefit in Your Child's Use of Social Media, Apps, and Digital Devices* (Guilford Press, 2015), 252.

[114] "Sleep and Sleep Disorders," *Centers for Disease Control and Prevention*, www.cdc.gov/sleep/about_sleep/how_much_sleep.html (accessed January 18, 2019).

[115] Homayoun, 165.

[116] Gold, 39.

[117] Homayoun, 167.

[118] Gold, 37-8.

[119] "How Online Predators Target Victims on Social Media," *Smart Social* (January 8, 2018), https://smartsocial.com/online-predators-social-media/ (accessed January 18, 2019).

[120] Christine Elgersma, "The Facts about Online Predators Every Parent Should Know," *Common Sense Media* (July 25, 2017), www.commonsensemedia.org/blog/the-facts-about-online-predators-every-parent-should-know (January 18, 2019).

[121] For detailed information on some of the most dangerous social networking apps, see Chad Landman, "The Most Dangerous Apps for Kids," *Out of Egypt: Liberation and Covenant in* Exodus (Freed-Hardeman University, 2019), 286-8, or go to https://smartsocial.com/.

[122] Aisling Moloney, "What is Kik Messenger and is it safe?" *Metro* (August 22, 2017), https://metro.co.uk/2017/08/22/what-is-kik-messenger-and-is-it-safe-6870370/ (accessed January 19, 2019).

[123] www.omegle.com.

[124] Jim Edwards, "The alleged betrayal in these photos, texts, and emails cost Snapchat $158 million," *Business Insider* (February 3, 2017), www.businessinsider.com/snapchat-founders-lawsuit-internal-photos-texts-emails-2017-2 (accessed January 21, 2019).

[125] "145 Snapchat Statistics, Facts and Figures (December 2018) by the Numbers," *DMR* (January 13, 2019), http://expandedramblings.com/index.php/snapchat-statistics/ (accessed January 19, 2019).

Chapter 12: Spiritual Health

[126] Tim Elmore, "Morality and Social Media: Have You Considered the Impact?" *Growing Leaders* (August 4, 2016), https://growingleaders.com/blog/morality-social-media-considered-impact/ (accessed September 7, 2018).

[127] Katherine Cross, "It's Not Just Logan Paul and YouTube – The Moral Compass of Social Media Is Broken," *The Verge* (January 4, 2018), www.theverge.com/2018/1/4/16850798/logan-paul-youtube-social-media-twitch-moderation (accessed September 7, 2018).

[128] Jonathan McKee, *The Teen's Guide to Social Media & Mobile Devices* (Shiloh Run Press, 2017), 62.

Chapter 13: Building a Social Media Contract

[129] John Stonestreet and Brett Kunkle, *A Practical Guide to Culture: Helping the Next Generation Navigate Today's World* (David C. Cook, 2017), loc 1358.

[130] "100 Distracted Driving Facts & Statistics for 2018," *Teen Safe* (April 5, 2018), www.teensafe.com/distracted-driving/100-distracted-driving-facts-and-statistics-2018/ (accessed January 22, 2019).

[131] Stonestreet and Kunkle, loc 1376.

also available through
Riddle Creek Publishing

To the Overcomers by Andy Kizer
Make Your Stand by Drew Kizer
Wisdom's Call by Drew Kizer
Be Wise God's Way by Adam Faughn
The Cast of the Cross by Drew Kizer
From Slaves to Conquerors by Barton Kizer
Marriage and the Christian Home by Dr. Ted Burleson
Who Knew? Records of Divine Providence by Andy Kizer
From Conquerors to Kings by Drew Kizer
From Captives to Christ by Drew Kizer
The Fifteen Periods of Bible History by Andy Kizer
Christian Hope by Drew Kizer
Christian Faith by Drew Kizer

Made in the USA
Coppell, TX
29 January 2023

11893322R00095